Merse Local Rhymes and Other Poems

In memory of
"Hendy"
George Henderson Fairbairn Turner
Joiner Cabinetmaker Millwright

Merse Local Rhymes and Other Poems
by
George Henderson
1800–1864

Edited with an Introduction
by
W. G. Henderson

ESKBANK BOOKS

Published by
Eskbank Books
29/2 Gilmour Road
Edinburgh

Typeset in Garamond 11/13 pt

Printed and bound in Great Britain by
CPI Antony Rowe

A CIP record for this book is available from
the British Library

ISBN 978 0 9562235 0 0

Contents

Other Poems

Acknowledgments

I would like to express my thanks to the many people who have given so generously of their time in the preparation of this book, and in particular:

Linda Bankier and Carole Pringle of the Record Office, Berwick-upon-Tweed.
The staff of the Scottish Border Archive at Selkirk and Hawick.
Dr Margaret Mackay and staff at The School of Scottish Studies.
Dr Lynn Clark of the Dept of Linguistics and English Language, University of Edinburgh.
Eddie Clark of Edinburgh University Press.
Ian Davidson of Edinburgh University Press.
Iain D. R. Henderson, for computer assistance.
Iseabail McLeod, for lexicographical advice.
My wife Jean, for patient support and wise counsel.

Introduction

In his anthology *Minstrelsy of the Merse*, published in 1893, the Rev. W. S. Crockett traced the rich contribution to the poetry and song of Scotland made by the writers of the eastern Borders, and particularly of Berwickshire. The arrangement is historical, beginning with Thomas of Ercildoune, the legendary Thomas the Rhymer. Many famous names follow, with songs and verses which will be widely familiar. However, it may be surprising, but relevant to this present book, that as an opening page Crockett chose an extract from George Henderson's early poem "The Return Home". This honour, he must have felt, was due to one he described later, as "a most notable man of the Merse". Crockett wrote:

> Of Dr. Henderson, more than any other Merse man, it must be said that he excelled in love for his native county, and was justly proud of its record in the nation's history. He laboured with indefatigable diligence to draw, from every possible source, any item of interest regarding it. His busy professional career brought him in contact with every phase of life, and, never losing sight of his first duty, he yet gathered an enormous accumulation of rare and curious facts relating to Berwickshire and its people. These, unfortunately, only exist in MS. Dr Henderson undoubtedly meant to publish much of this collection, but the opportunity for his doing so never came. Besides many newspaper articles, his only work in book form is the well-known "Popular Rhymes, Proverbs, and Sayings of the County of Berwick," published at Newcastle in 1856.
>
> As a poet he takes a good rank. His powers in this direction are seen to the greatest advantage in the descriptions of

> Merse scenery and life, that flow with such rare beauty and deftness of expression from his facile pen. He is equally at home in the harvest-field, the heathered moorland, or the grey hillside, and he loves to sing in pleasing idylls of the country and its charms.

In fact, Dr George Henderson did publish at least two other books of verse, which had limited circulation and are now very scarce. One of these, *Scenes of Boyhood and Other Poems*, is reproduced in facsimile form in this volume (see pp. 159–218). The preface to this makes it clear that George Henderson had a modest view of his own poetic abilities and would have been embarrassed by Crockett's praise:

> I claim for myself no elevated walk in the regions of Poetry. I am content to be thought of as one who delights to wander about the skirts of the Parnassian hill – and I shall not be disappointed to see others walking in a higher sphere, and basking in the sunshine of popular favour: – yet the lowly violet shows not unlovely beneath the shade of the peerless rose, or the stately fox-glove. My theme is local, and I have no wish that my name should extend beyond the locality of which I sing.

It is hoped, however, that this present collection will confirm Crockett's view rather than Dr Henderson's own. Most of the poems here have been gathered from the pages of the *Berwick Advertiser*, which had the admirable habit of publishing a regular poetry column. This was itself a mark of the importance that poetry enjoyed at that time, when local newspapers were in their infancy and space was at a premium. The series of Merse Local Rhymes have been kept together, because they were in that group which Dr Henderson kept promising, but was unable to deliver as a volume on its own. The other poems have been presented in the date order in which they were written. No attempt has been made to arrange them by subject matter and they thus reflect the author's changing interests over the years.

George Henderson, 1800–1864

George Henderson was born on May 5, 1800 in the old farmhouse of Little Billy, in the parish of Bunkle, near Chirnside in Berwickshire. He was the eldest son of John Henderson and his wife Frances Purves, both families having deep roots in the eastern Borders of Scotland. Little Billy with its neighbours Billy Hill and Billy Mill formed a group of small farming communities taking their names from the ancient Billy Castle whose ruins lie nearby. They were about to vanish in the course of the agricultural improvements then in progress – now frequently described as the Lowland Clearances. These circumstances were a significant influence in George's life and work. His early years were spent in close contact with a peasant life which was relatively poor materially, but rich in traditions and folklore which he came to value deeply.

George's initial education was at a local school whch deserves credit for nourishing this "lad o' pairts". From his earliest years, he was obviously observant, imaginative and impressionable and the environment in which he was growing up was just what was needed to feed those faculties. His daily walk to school took him past the ruins of Billy Castle and he later wrote, in his unpublished journals:

> although I then knew nothing of its history, yet many a time I roamed around its shattered towers with a strange and undefined curiosity, musing on the times and men of old and half afraid lest some ancient warrior should stalk from behind the mouldering walls and confront me sword in hand and armed to the teeth with coat of mail and with helmet and habergeon on.

That was the start of a lifelong interest in local history and in the archaeological remains with which the district abounds. Natural history was equally appealing:

> In life's early morn, how often have I plucked the ladies smock, pilewort and primrose by the marsh-bordered rills and green mounds around the lonely ruins of Billy, and I well remember,

> though at a distance of more than 30 years, plucking the vernal flowers on the mossy banks and listening with delight to the voice of the cuckoo re-echoing through the venerable trees that enclose its decaying walls. … From that day to the present we have had a strong and increasing desire to visit ancient castles, churches, monuments and battlefields and a delight in prying into their origin and history although it be only fragments that we can at any time pick up.

It was this picking up of fragments that would lead eventually to the publication of his best-known work *The Popular Rhymes, Sayings, and Proverbs of the County of Berwick.*

Around 1812 came the traumatic changes that saw the destruction of Little Billy and its community and the incorporation of the farm and its small neighbours into the larger unit of Billy Mains. George's father moved to the tenancy of the farm of Greenhead, near to Auchencrow where George continued his education at the school, Grammar Hall, which had a high reputation, having been founded by John Strauchan, an eminent Greek and Latin scholar, who was succeeded by John Boag, a congregational preacher and author of a large *Dictionary of the English Language.* That rigorous schooling laid the foundation for his later university education and fed a breadth of interest which was to be reflected in the extensive library that he built up throughout his life.

A biographical note in a verse anthology, *The Modern Scottish Minstrel*, by Charles Rogers, tells us that he entered the University of Edinburgh when he was in his nineteenth year to study English, but that "after the close of his second session, he temporarily abandoned literary pursuits". What caused this surprising retreat is not explained. However, we do know that there were family problems at home. His much loved elder sister Helen, the subject of two poems in this collection – "The Maid of Danskein" and "Helen" – married and died tragically young around that time. His father had also suffered a serious accident which perhaps made George's presence at home desirable. Whatever the reason, it is obvious from his later life that he was not willing to give up literature, and in particular poetry.

By 1825 George was back at Edinburgh University, this time with the intention of studying medicine. He seems to have attended only one class, in chemistry, before transferring to the Royal College of Surgeons of Edinburgh. This change was not unusual at the time and was apparently a less expensive option. It was an interesting period in the teaching of medicine and surgery. In 1826 the College of Surgeons made a course of three months of practical surgery compulsory and the University followed suit. It was this that led to the great increase in demand for bodies for dissection, which spurred on the resurrectionists, most famously in the case of Burke and Hare.

George became a Licentiate of the College of Surgeons in March 1829, having passed their examinations in anatomy, surgery and pharmacy. He lost no time in returning to Chirnside to set himself up in practice as a surgeon. By July of that year, with great self-belief and missionary enthusiasm he was writing to *The Lancet* to expose what he described as "quackery in Berwickshire". He wrote:

> As you have always been most ready to expose corruption and empiricism in all its forms, it is the intention of this paper to lay open a system of impudent quackery, which has long prevailed in this neighbourhood, to the great detriment and annoyance of the regulars of the surrounding country. It has grown to an extent quite unequalled in the annals of medicine, and yet no one has had the courage to make the attempt of crushing the many-headed Gorgon.

Stern stuff indeed, and one might think foolhardy. How it was greeted by his professional colleagues we do not know, but it was early evidence of his uncompromising style in matters about which he felt strongly. He went on to give detailed examples of the iniquities of the quackery of the man he called "the little fat doctor of Dunse", in a way that nowadays would have been inviting litigation.

It is a source of great frustration that we know so little about Dr George's medical practice. What has survived of his writing, in his published works and in transcripts of manuscripts, suggests that his other interests, in local history and customs, botany and particularly in poetry, must have taken up all his free time. Most disappointing of all, is the fact that a journal that he later kept, of a year in his life as a country doctor has disappeared. This was the subject of an article in the journal *Medical History* (Vol. V 1961), by Dr W. S. Mitchell, formerly librarian of the University of Newcastle upon Tyne, who had had it on loan from one of Dr George's grandsons. Mitchell described it as: "in two volumes, totalling 653 pages, bound in half calf, lettered *Nugae medici*, and with the ticket of George Johnston, Murray Street, Dunse". It was last seen by family descendants in the late 1960s and was sold to an unknown buyer. Extensive searches have failed to find it, but it is to be hoped that it may yet turn up.

Certainly, the quotations from it given by Dr Mitchell are intriguing and give valuable insights into Dr George's beliefs and prejudices. His passion for collecting information about local customs and beliefs led him to describe many folk cures. Some of his views would strike us as admirably modern: he hated smoking, loathed the abuse of alcohol and would have been a vegetarian, had his wife allowed.

But, of his daily practice we know very little. For thirty-five years he attended to the needs of patients in and around Chirnside, riding out on horseback as required, at all hours and in all weathers over a wide area. That his mind was not only on medical matters, is illustrated by this quotation from his memoirs:

> When riding by night, either to or from my patients, I find it a good plan, to prevent me from wearying on the journey, to keep repeating some piece of poetry. On coming home this morning I repeated aloud for many times, Addison's beautiful hymn "The spacious firmament on high", etc. "Tam o' Shanter" is an excellent poem to recite on a night journey, also Gray's "Elegy", Thomson's "Hymn on the Seasons" etc. Such an exercise keeps you warm and comfortable. In a rough tempestuous night it is particularly pleasant to recite aloud some sublime strain of the olden time. I would recommend every country surgeon to commit to memory one at least of the books of Milton's "Paradise Lost" – and use it as a stimulus in a cold night journey.

On his rounds, Dr George was also able to follow his other interests and in 1831 he became one of the founder members of the Berwickshire Naturalists' Club, which continues to this day. He made significant contributions to its journal and throughout his life kept up a correspondence with its leading members, particularly on botanical matters.

In April 1837 he married Margaret Hood, daughter of Robert Hood, tailor in Chirnside. He was thirty-seven, she seventeen. It was a marriage that would last some twenty-seven years, producing thirteen pregnancies, though only seven children survived to adulthood; itself a commentary on the fragility of life and the limited powers of a doctor in those days. The marriage was what was called "irregular", in that it was a civil ceremony at a marriage house at Lamberton Toll on the Scottish/English Border. Such weddings were quite common at that time, particularly among those who were dissenters from the established church, as we know was the case with this branch of the Hendersons and also the Hoods.

Their first child, Agnes, was born on February 15, 1838, but, sadly, died in October 1839 of whooping cough, a common cause of childhood death at that time and yet another reminder of the fragility of life. Her brief life and tragic death is the subject of the poem, "Stanzas to the Memory of my First-born", which appears in Dr George's first book, *Scenes of Boyhood and Other Poems*, published privately, in 1840.

Scenes of Boyhood and Other Poems is now so scarce that a facsimile reprint of it has been included in this volume. The "Prefatory Epistle to a Friend", with which that book begins, is a valuable statement of his views on the social and religious issues of his time and place, well worth having as a background to his work. The long title poem is a touching evocation of the lost world of his childhood as well as an expression of anger at the changes wrought in the name of agricultural improvement.

This must have been a period of great literary activity for the Doctor, because the book closes with a list of no less than six other works that he says are "ready for the Press". None of these ever appeared as advertised, but they contain the first mention of the "Proverbs, Rythmes, &c. peculiar to the County" which he was gathering. He also mentions antiquarian and botanical excursions, the products of which he shared with colleagues in the Berwickshire Naturalists' Club.

The breadth of his reading, as revealed in his personal library, was quite striking. He built up a collection of some 2,500 volumes of which only a small part was related to his medical practice. Literature, and particularly poetry, figured prominently alongside natural history, folklore, history both ancient and modern, religion, philosophy and classical works in Greek and Latin

Along with his medical practice, he had a growing family to deal with. A second daughter, Fanny, born just after the death of Agnes in 1839 happily survived and must have been some consolation. His first son, John followed in 1842. A Robert who died in infancy was born in 1844 and, as was customary at the time, the name was used again for a second Robert (Robert Hood) in 1845. A second Agnes (Agnes Renton) followed in 1850, then George in 1853, Thomas William in 1855, and James Simpson in 1858. Two more boys, Alexander in 1861 and Ebenezer in 1863, both died in infancy.

The Popular Rhymes, Sayings, and Proverbs of the County of Berwick, the product of so many years of collccting and commenting, was published in 1856. Although now scarce, it is regarded as an important source of customs and folklore and is likely to be found in libraries wherever there are Scots. Characteristically, he could not resist including a few poems of his own, of local interest. The title page describes him as "Author of 'Winter Rhymes, etc. etc.'" and his Preface regrets that:

> we are only sorry that we have been unable to introduce, as it was our intention to have done, a number of original Local Rhymes, which want of space alone compels us to omit. But should we be spared health and leasure, many of these pieces may find a niche in a much more extended publication…

This "extended publication" in book form never appeared in his lifetime, and it is to remedy that fact that this present collection was conceived.

Winter Rhymes, which had been published by the Berwick bookseller A. Henderson, was favourably reviewed in the *Berwick Advertiser* in January 1856:

> His observation of nature is constant and exact; and especially does he delight in local subjects, around which he gathers all traditional and historical interest, and to which he gives the colouring of his cheerful and buoyant mind. We could

> have wished that he had given us a volume of his Merse Local Rhymes, and hope that the success of his present small venture will encourage him to make a larger collection at an early period.

The *Berwick Advertiser* took up its own suggestion by publishing *Merse Local Rhymes*, as a numbered series of twenty, in its regular poetry column. Many of them relate to the local traditional tales and customs which are dealt with in *The Popular Rhymes, Sayings, and Proverbs*. The last in the series, published on November 15, 1856, was accompanied by a note:

> As the health of the writer of these rhymes has been, for some time past, in a precarious state, this will likely be the last of the series that will appear in these columns.

In fact, there were quite a lot of poems to come. These are presented in the "Other Poems" section of this book.

The last seven years of George's life were marred by ill-health and some financial difficulties. An interesting letter to the Editor of the *Berwick Advertiser*, published in 1854, had set out in detail one year's income and expenses which showed a small loss, attributable mainly to the failure of patients to pay their bills:

> A great portion of what the doctor does receive, in the way of fees, is grudgingly and scantily paid – and much of it is got only by constant dunning and with great difficulty. In these statements it will be seen that the Dissenting Minister who has one hundred pounds a year of stipend, a rent free house and garden and no horse to keep, is four times better off as regards worldly circumstances than the doctor – and that the parochial teacher with seventy pounds a year, garden and house, is twice as well off as him. It may be that the medical person who makes this statement is much worse paid than his medical brethren – he sometimes thinks so. He has been nearly thirty years in practice with no better success than what this account shows. He is not inclined to complain, loves his profession – and wishes to

> do good to to his fellow mortals – nothing can break him down but ill health, of which he has a constant and considerable share; but he is still determined to prosecute his calling to the utmost of his ability – and "die in harness" if no better can be.

Characteristically, this letter used his personal experience on behalf of his fellow practitioners. He goes on to point out that in the previous twenty-five years, fifteen doctors in the county died "in absolute poverty or in very distressed circumstances" and that of these fifteen, three committed suicide. A further fourteen, at least, had left the county because they could not make a livelihood in it. Only some half dozen had been successful: "that is to say, two or three have died above want – and other two or three are in comfortable circumstances, and are in a condition to save a little for infirmity, or old age."

Unfortunately, infirmity rather than old age was to be George's lot. The poetry continued, though it may not be too fanciful to detect an increasing nostalgia and awareness of mortality.

Another curious and interesting literary venture has recently come to light. In 1862 translations into "Lowland Scotch" of The Song of Solomon and The Gospel of St Matthew, from the Authorised English Version, were published. There is some reason to believe that these were by this particular George Henderson. They were privately printed in very limited editions for Louis-Lucien Bonaparte the comparative linguist and dialectologist, as part of a series of some twenty versions of the same texts which he had commissioned in local dialects ranging from Cornwall to Shetland. The translation of Matthew's Gospel has a preface written in what seems very like Dr George's characteristic style and is signed off in his customary way with plain initials, G. H. There was correspondence between Bonaparte and his translators which might confirm the authorship , but so far this has not been found.

In the end, Dr George did have his wish to die in harness. The following notice appeared in the *Berwick Advertiser* of July 9, 1864:

CHIRNSIDE – Our village has sustained a severe loss this week in the death of Dr. Henderson. For some time past he had felt symptoms of incipient paralysis, but with his usual reserve said little about them. A fortnight ago the disease assumed a more decided form, and in a short time his left side was completely paralysed. From the first he seemed to think that his end was not distant, and though everything that the skill of three of his brethren could suggest was done for him he became gradually worse and expired on Monday evening the 4th instant. Three weeks ago he was going out and in among us, apparently in his usual health, and now he is gone, and the place that has known him so long shall know him no more. As he lived he died, an unassuming sincere Christian. Though his sufferings were very great before his death he uttered no word of repining, but bowed submissively to the will of God. His somewhat sudden removal has created a wide spread and deep feeling of sorrow. "He will be much missed", "He was a good poor man's doctor", are the words that come first to the lips of all that speak of him. Though only 64 years of age, the fatigue and exposure of a 35 years practice had given him the appearance of an older man. He was a man of gentle manners, tender sympathies, refined tastes, and excellent mental powers. To a great love of antiquarian lore, a large stock of which he had acquired, he united no small measure of the practice gift. He had a quick eye and a keen relish for all the beauties of nature, and loved to reproduce them in his poems; and these prove that he was no mere rhymer, but a genuine poet. Many a heavy ride was beguiled in their composition. The early primroses, or the homeless wanderer exposed to winter's storms, would make the fire burn, and the poem would be finished ere he reached his home. The public is not aware, and perhaps never will be, of the loss it has sustained by his death, for his retiring disposition did not allow him to do justice to his powers. With these few imperfect words we bid farewell to a brave true spirit that has gone to his rest and reward.

Dr George was buried, as he had wished, in the graveyard of Chirnside Parish Church, beside his parents and other family members. A prominent memorial, close to the west end of the church marks the place and bears the inscription:

Erected in beloved remembrance of Geo. Henderson
Surgeon for 35 years in Chirnside
Who died 4th July 1864 aged 64 years
Well remembered for his universal kindness and benevolence

It is not known who was responsible for the erection of this monument, which is much grander than the family circumstances would have suggested. It would be nice to think that the local community had some hand in it.

Certainly the relative poverty that he had complained about seems to have been confirmed by the fact that his precious library was put up for sale by auction before the year was out. The sale catalogue, which casts an interesting light on the width of his lifetime's reading, carried an appeal:

> As the Books are to be sold for the benefit of the late Dr Henderson's family, it is hoped that friends and acquaintances in the district, as well as the public generally, will patronise the Sale.

The sale took place in the Town Hall, Dunse on December 15 and 16, 1864. There is no record of the amount raised.

Dr George's widow Margaret lived on in Chirnside for another thirty years, until her death, aged 74 on December 26, 1894. She was at that time living with her son Robert Hood Henderson and his wife at Rowan Tree House, where Robert practised as the local chemist. Robert,who was much respected, was the last of the sons to remain in Chirnside, until he died in 1915.

Merse Local Rhymes

The Witches of Edencraw

"In the town o' Edencraw
Where the witches bide a'"
Old Rhyme

In langsyne days in ancient times,
When rang in Britain's isle King James,
Then witches wraught their awfu' crimes
In mony a house and ha',
'Mang thae were foremost say auld rhymes,
The witches o' Edencraw.

They play'd wild pranks in bught and fauld,
Round wechts in barns they danced bauld,
In mirksome howes they reel'd and squall'd,
And frightened great and sma',
And mony a saul to death they haul'd –
The witches o' Edencraw.

Wi' gley'd laird Borgue they met and danc'd
And 'bout the bour trees nightly pranced;
Wi' carl cats they squeeled and ranc'd
Round the old bastle's wa',
And in the dark their wild e'en glanc'd –
The witches o' Edencraw.

They witch'd complete laird Bogue's auld mare
That she wad neither gang nor steer;
As she cam down the loan wi' bere
She flang the laird and a'.
And they maist made him swarf wi' fear
The witches o' Edencraw.

As Robin Rae cam hame we saut
He saw a hare as grey's his hat
Rin cross his path, and there he swat –
For fear he maist did fa';
For oft was seen like hare or cat
The witches o' Edencraw.

The gudewife's butter wadna kirn,
The gudewife's milk it wadna yirn;
And troth they play'd a bonny pirn
On decent Nelly Shaw,
They chang'd her wool to clotts o' shairn –
The witches o' Edencraw.

A' night they plew'd the Windy flat
Wi' thirteen paddocks and a rat
Yok'd in a pleugh – auld Nick held that,
Seven warlocks did it ca';
And on the knowe a' girnin' sat
The witches o' Edencraw.

A feast was held in Buncle kirk,
Whereat was wrought some fearfu' wark
Wi' imps o' ill, wha like the dark
And spurn the auld gude law;
And rudous wives – grim, gaunt and stark –
The witches o' Edencraw.

Out o' their graves, below the stanes,
They houkit skulls wi' grievous granes,
And wrought their cantrips owre the banes,
Mischief 'mang men to saw –
A wicked crew, as ilk man kens –
The witches o' Edencraw.

Neist day the corn was blown to labbs
Three boats gaed down, right aff St Abbs,
And lang and sair, in fitful sabs,
The wind did furious blaw;
Yet merrily gaed the spitefu' gabs
O' the witches o' Edencraw.

John Bonner's house was driven doun;
Poor John had got out wi' cracked crown,
They hadna power to smoor or drown
That honest man ava;
And he got free o' ilka loon,
'Mang witches o' Edencraw.

Some o' thae hags they burn'd to dead
High up on Shielupdikes knowe-head,
And some *aboon the breath* did bleed
In yonder reeky raw;
For in a' ill they took the lead,
The witches o' Edencraw.

But at the length some light arose,
And not a witch durst show her nose;
Meg Girvan's days in storm did close –
She was the last o' a';
And ne'er again will be our foes
The witches o' Edencraw.

Wi"s Greek and Latin, Strauchon[1] came,
Thae ill gien witches a' to tame,
And Boag shed light on mony a hame
Frae his auld Grammar Ha';
But now they're only ken'd in raeme,
The witches o' Edencraw.

And now, on earth, nae witch surpasses
Siller, drink, and bonny lasses;
They witch wise men and silly asses
To mony a fatal fa',
And bring on us far waur distresses
Than witches o' Edencraw.

Chirnside, May 14, 1855. H.
Merse Local Rhymes, No. 1.

[1] *Strauchon and Boag were schoolmasters in Edencraw.*

Edencraw was the old name for the present village of Auchencrow, where George Henderson went to school. The line about bleeding "aboon the breath" refers to the belief that scoring the forehead of a witch with the mark of the Cross destroyed her evil powers. Ed.

Jock o' the Myre

Billy Myre (once an impassable morass, now drained, lying along the northern boundary of Chirnside parish) has long been the haunt of a fearful ghost, called "Jock o' the Myre".

In yon deep morass, low under the knowe,
The paddocks were croupin' down i' the howe;
In the black peat holes, a' slimy and caller,
The filthy asks and taeds did waller;
And the grey saugh-bushes were dimly seen,
Wi reeds, and seggs, and humlocks green,
When Jock o' the Myre, at the midnight hour,
Through the wreaths o' mist did gape and glower.

The folk did slummer in cot and ha',
And fearin' dreams did dummer them a';
On the Pyper knowe thick waved the broom,
And alang a' the howe lay a misty gloom;
On ilka side a' the hills were dry,
Nae dew that night did fa' frae the sky –
For ay when Jock o' the Myre is seen
A' nature is chill'd wi' his glarin' een!

The moon did waver deep i' the cluds,
The blast was soughin' wi' dreary thuds,
The blitter did cry ower the bog aboon,
The bull on the brae did eerie croon;
And owre the tap o' the Craigish-law
A shadow o' gloom did darkly fa' –
Then Jock o' the Myre, by the Causey stane,
Came sloomin' alang wi' a waefu' maen.

The sheep in the fauld – the kye in the loan,
Did shudder and quake, and start and groan;
The thunder mutter'd far i' the west,
The lightnin' glanc'd frae the mountain's crest;
And down i' the Nunbutts, deeply down,

'Twas dark as pitch – or Gomorrah town –
When Jock o' the Myre look'd through the dark,
A' wrapped around in a bluidy sark!

That fearfu' night, Watt Haig i' the Shiel
To Bullerhead gaed, wampussin' weel,
To court his Marion – his love, and jo,
And gain'd her consent to bundle and go;
But wanderin' hame, he tint the gate,
And plung'd in the hole like a muckle skate: –
And Jock o' the Myre did guller and grane,
To see him sink by the Causey stane!

As hame frae the fair, to Moormountrig,
Tam Todd came stacherin' by the brig,
He slipped and fit and owre did fa'
And fell i' the slough owre head and a';
Sair, sair he struggled to get to the land,
But the reeds and rushes brak i' his hands: –
And Jock o' the Myre did owre him gape,
And bore him down wi' his awesome shape!

Queer Will-o'-the Wisp was glimmerin' dim,
By the wild saugh-buss, on the deep hag's rim;
When reckless Habbie o' Howburn Mill
Came stoiterin' down the Oldcastles hill;
He took the light for some cottage bole,
And stumbled into a black peat hole; –
There Jock o' the Myre did haud him fast,
And he ne'er gat out o' the glarry cast.

Soon, soon i' the mornin', frae his maid,
Will Aikmen down frae Mayfield gaed;
And ay as he sang owre Billy Moor –
"O, my Margery's heart I'm unco sure,
And the neist time I cross Draedan burn
I'll hae her consent before I turn!" –
But Jock o' the Myre was watchin' weel,
And he ne'er got back to Margery Steele!

Frae Edencraw, auld coalman Pete
Ae night drank lang wi' yell-wife Kate;
And ay as he stoited frae side tae side
He thought o' her siller wi' muckle pride –
"And, troth! her posy will make me strang,
I'll hae a farm ere it be lang!"
But Jock o' the Myre tript up his heels,
And low he lies 'mang paddocks and eels!

O Jock o' the Myre is an unco ghaist,
He frightens the dominie, doctor, and priest;
He frightens the miller, when drinkin' his mooter,
He frightens the wabster, tailor, and sutor;
He startles the rogue and loon on their path,
And holds to their view the vision o' death; –
O could he but gar a' the folk gang right,
We'd bear, now and then, his horrible sight.

I've been eerie mysel' at the midnight mirk,
When todlin' hame frae some weary wark,
To cross the Myre at the Causey brae,
When the mist and the gloom on the deep howe lay,
When the gleam o' the bog-fire hover'd nigh,
And not a star was seen i' the sky –
Then Jock o' the Myre seemed coming on,
And wi' horror my heart was overthrown!

O Jock o' the Myre is a fearfu' ghaist!
O Jock o' the Myre is an awfu' pest! –
He frightens the bairns and lads at e'en;
And wae to the wight wha his form has seen,
Wi' his throat frae lug to lug cut deep,
And his face as white as a new-wash'd sheep!
Ye'd better wade ay through waeter and fire
Than meet lang Jock o' the Billy Myre!

Chirnside, May 31, 1855. H.
Merse Local Rhymes, No. 2.

The Fairies o' Fosterland

"Fairy elves,
Where midnight revels by a forest side,
Or fountain, some belated peasant sees,
Or dreams he sees."
Paradise Lost

"The fairy folk o' Fosterland,
The witches o' Edencraw."
Old Rhyme

When bonny Mary illustrious shone,
And held the sceptre on Scotia's throne;
When warriors grim held castle and town,
And mail clad troopers up and down
The Borderside, and the moorland dells,
And reivers rude came over the fells –
Then tript in many a lichtsome band
The lovely fairies o' Fosterland.

Sweet were their pipings, sweet and shrill,
Heard at midnight on Mayfield hill;
And down by the burn, the camp below,
They tript o'er the green in many a row:
Or sat at their feast, near the upland well,
Where blossomed yellow the asphodel;
Or round the ring a' hand in hand,
Danc'd the blithe fairies o' Fosterland.

On the blae-berry bank the moon shone bright,
And the heather bells hung fair i' th' light;
And the red moss-cup, and the lichen grey,
Were spread aboon on the dewy brae;
In murmurs sweet the burn flow'd on,
And rippled around the glitty stone;
And a' down the Merse the view was grand,
To the fairy-folk o' the Fosterland.

Frae crystal cups o' the diamond fine,
They drank wi' joy their blaeberry wine;
And sweetest fruits o' ilk taste and hue
Were heap'd on baskets o' green and blue,
And apples, and nuts, and berries red,
On the dewy leaves were profusely spread –
O gladsome feast by the fountain strand,
And happy the fairies o' Fosterland.

Sic lovely forms never were seen,
As trod that night the gowany green;
And the Elfin Queen the feast did crown,
Wi' Thomas, the harper o' Ercildoun.
True Thomas sat there among them a'
The sweetest harper the warld e'er saw –
And ay he harp'd at the Queen's command
To the lovely fairies o' Fosterland.

Through a' the forest the music rang,
On Buncle hills and moors alang,
While the wind slept still, and soft and clear
The moonbeams glimmer'd far and near;
In bower, and cottage, and lordly ha'
Sweet dreams and slumbers fell on them a' –
For owre a' was waved a magic wand,
While feasted the fairies o' Fosterland.

A' gliding along on the lunar rays
There came elfin bands frae Alewater braes;
Frae the long yellow broom on the Piper knowes,
And the Cradle-knowes, where the Whitadder flows,
Came bonny green trains in their blithe array;
Ilk Border dean, and ilk Border brae,
Sent forth that night a green-clad band,
To feast wi' the fairies o' Fosterland.

By the camps and cairns along the hill
They went and came a' that midnight still:
Frae Ordweil-brae, 'boon the Strait-loup spout,
And frae pastoral Quixwood they a' came out,
On their palfrey's white a' riding along,
While far down the plain some reapers sang,
Frae the kirn gaen hame, was echoing bland,
And rejoiced the fairies o' Fosterland.

When rank'd on the rigs are the harvest stooks,
And the rustlin' barley a' mellow looks;
When sweet fa's the gloamin' and dewy shower
O'er the slopes and howes o' the Lammermoor,
Then to the elfin bands 'tis very sweet
In the mossy dells wi' their Queen to meet –
And many a time, in many a band,
Met the fairy-folk o' the Fosterland.

Since the days when Wallace, that knight sae true,
The freedom o' Scotland did thrice rescue;
And since the Bruce, at the Bannockburn,
Proud Edward's host did a' overturn –
The fairies hae been the pride o' our dells,
Our woods and braes, and crystaline wells;
And i' the faith and charms we'll ever stand
O' the fairy-folk o' the Fosterland.

It is said they hae fled fra ilk green knowe
Sin' they were torn by the sock o' the plough;
It is said they hae gaen frae ilk dean and brae,
Sin' tea and potatoes came here away;
And never mair at the midsummer e'en
They'll dance by the burn or the dewy green;
They're gane for ay! and new times hae dawn'd
On the fairy-folk o' the Fosterland.

They're a' away frae the Border-side,
New manners and customs they canna 'bide;
The auld pastoral days o' out sires are gane,
And wi' braw new comers they canna remain;
To the Elfin land, far ower sea and firth
They'll take nae mair bairns o' mortal birth –
And now to us they'll be nae mair ken'd
The fairy-folk o' the Fosterland.

Chirnside, June, 1855. H.
Merse Local Rhymes, No. 3.

◇◇◇◇◇◇◇◇

John o' the Bank

About 60 or 70 years ago, a farmer resided at Blackadder Bank in the parish of Edrom, who was called by himself, or by his neighbours – "Fair and Honest John o' the Bank." He seems, if these lines give anything like a fair representation of his character, to have been a kind of second edition of "John o' Badenyond."

There is mony a man who has wonderfu' brags
'Bout his sheep, and his nowte, his kye, and his nags;
At fair and at market they blaw and they boast
O' what they hae gain'd – but ne'er what they've lost: –
I carena a button for a' sic palavers,
There's unco sma' truth in boastin' and havers;
And I'll yield to nae man whate'er be his rank,
For fair and honest I'll ay be – John o' the Bank!

Wi' their wild spankin' fillies a dike they may loup,
And through gude corn land may canter and scoup;
Wi' red coats like jockeys then bum unco fast,
Though their canterin' leads them oft into some cast,
Let them ride! – I'll ay keep the crown o' the causey
On my ain steady aiver – a decent auld bausie;
And I'll haud ay the gully right by the shank,
For fair and honest I'll aye be – John o' the Bank!

We've unco braw folk now at market and kirk,
Wi' gumflowers and ribbons to hide ilka lirk;
They're a' buskit bonny frae head to the heel,
And vain as the peacock wi' bright gaudy tail –
But were the truth kenn'd ay, we'd find it was such,
That merchant and tailor were oft left i' th' lurch,
And we've often seen proud folk come down wi' a clank,
But fair and honest I'll aye be – John o' the Bank!

There are some folks gang cringin' and sneakin' along,
And beckin' and bowin' to rich and to strong –
Wi' low groflin' spirit let them slave i' the dust,
In goodness and virtue they hae but sma' trust;
They follow a' the fashions, devoted and keen,
And custom's auld errors hae blinded their een: –
Let them groffle away, and sink down i' the stank, –
But fair and honest I'll aye be – John o' the Bank!

They may vaunt o' their creeds, their kirk and their state,
But I'll haud aye my ain notions whate'er be my fate;
I maun look wi' my ain een or no see ava',
And judge what is solid frae what's a mere blaw;
There are thousands rin daft after priests and sic like,
But in prayin' and preachin' there's mony a slee tike,
That wears a fair cloak with the good anes to rank –
But fair and honest I'll aye be – John o' the Bank!

To gain a bit favour, some lie and some fawn,
And try mony schemes to accomplish a plan;
Some cheat and supplant, and backbite and sneer,
And murder your good name when nae friend is near;
The poison o' serpents is under their tongue,
And their lips wi' fell venom for ever are hung;
Pits for their neighbours they houk deep and dank –
But fair and honest I'll aye be – John o' the Bank!

Frae horse-couper louns, gude keep a' honest leivers!
And fair-sayin' birkies are as oft great deceivers;
They're sure to begouk ye wi' boastin' and blawin',
But will fine buskit promises pay what they are awin'?
To safety and peace there is only ae road,
And that's where truth and honesty hae their abode;
Then let a' clever aivers and grand fallows spank,
But fair and honest I'll aye be – John o' the Bank!

They may bouse at their whiskey, their wine, and their yill,
But gude caller water's the best o' drink still,
It keeps the head clear, and the heart leal and sound,
And ne'er throws a man, like a sow, on the ground;
Their grandeur and wealth are but a vain show,
Their greed and their grasping brings mony ane low;
And when they think to get prizes 'twill prove but a blank,
But fair and honest I'll aye be – John o' the Bank.

Chirnside, June, 1855. H.
Merse Local Rhymes, No. 4.

◇◇◇◇◇◇◇

Martha's Dream

The waning moon at midnight still
 Shower'd down her beams so deadly pale;
The mist wreathes hung on War-law hill,
 And shrouded a' the *Merse's* vale, –

When weary, stretch'd in calm repose,
 Fair Martha, o' yon hamlet, lay;
And wi' a heart o' many woes
 Her fancy wandered far away.

She thought upon her lover dear,
 In warlike vesture marching slow,
Where Crimean mountains, wild and drear,
 Rose in their copse o' frozen snow.

And slumber came and soothed her breast,
  And stayed the trickling briny tear;
The visions sad stole on her rest,
  And far she wandered, full o' fear.

She dream'd, and saw the fierce array
  Of hostile troops in conflict dire, –
'Twas Alma's glory battle day
  Shrouded in smoke and bursts of fire.

The warrior's shout, the thundering rout,
  The charging host of men and horse,
Pass'd in her view, green, red, and blue,
  All driven along with rapid force!

Clos'd was that scene – but quick again
  Another vision dim she sees,
All through the mist that wreath'd the plain
  Dark banners floated on the breeze.

And there she saw her lover stand,
  Amidst a throng of warriors stout,
Fierce fighting with a bloody hand,
  Against the Russian savage rout.

They fled before his powerful thrust;
  But while the victory loud was peal'd
He wounded fell, and sank in dust,
  On Inkermann's blood drenched field.

She saw him fall, and ran to save
  The soldier to her bosom dear;
But hurried to his deep red grave,
  He from her sight did disappear!

And cold the rain beat on her breast,
  While sitting lonely by his mound;
And weeping sore, the soil she press'd,
  Where lay her lover in the ground.

She woke in woe – while dawning grey
  Did through her cottage lattice stream;
And ere the gloamin o' the day
  She heard the news that rede her dream.

O doleful news! O doleful hour,
  That laid her manly Willie low!
When clouds and storms did fearful lour
  On Inkermann's sad vale o' woe.

O dreadful War! What woes are thine!
  What thousands thou hast made to weep;
What widows sigh! What orphans pine;
  Beneath thy fell, remorseless sweep!

What thousands too, like Martha fair,
  Are doom'd to mourn their lovers slain!
And driven to feel those pangs o' care
  That makes this life one scene o' pain!

Chirnside, August 13, 1855. H.
Merse Local Rhymes, No. 5.

We'll Meet Nae Mair by Draedan Burn

We'll meet nae mair by Draedan burn
When streaks the skies the harvest morn;
Nor in the dewy clover sweet
We'll bathe our field-ward going feet;
Nor see our labour just begun,
The sickles glitter in the sun
Among the rigs o' mellow corn –
Nae mair we'll meet by Draedan burn.

Nae mair we'll meet by Draedan burn,
Wi' maidens blythe as e'er were born,
To tedd the hay, or lint to steep
Down in the moss-holes dark and deep;
The holes are drain'd – the saugh-buss grey,
The bog-reeds tall in plum'd array,
And red moss flowers, are a' uptorn –
Nae mair we'll meet by Draedan burn.

Nae mair we'll meet by Draedan burn
The sheep to herd, the kye to turn;
The green burr-reed and meadow queen,
That o'er the rill waved morn and een,
We'll pu' nae mair, nor rashes plet
To form the sword or coronet;
Ah me! my heart is sair forlorn –
We'll meet nae mair by Draedan burn.

We'll meet nae mair by Draedan burn –
Though o'er past scenes the heart may yearn,
And grieve for they who once were there,
Toiling in hope and prospects fair
The patriarch sire, the mother dear.
Sisters and brothers void o' fear –
They're a' away ne'er to return –
We'll meet nae mair by Draedan burn.

By Draedan burn we'll meet nae mair,
The minnon or the loach to snare;
Or paidle in the stream wi' glee,
Or chase the gilded fly or bee;
Or lie beside the mossy knowe,
Where wav'd the hair grass o'er our brow,
Ah me! we hae much cause to mourn –
We'll meet nae mair by Draedan burn.

We'll meet nae mair by Draedan burn,
Nor scramble round yon hoary cairn,
Where ancient warriors nameless rot,
Their deeds of glory all forgot;
Nae mair we'll come the meadow by,
Where rosy milk maids milk the kye,
And sing the Forest Flowers forlorn –
Nae mair we'll meet by Draedan burn.

We'll meet nae mair by Draedan burn –
We're wandering further frae the morn;
And as we track our onward way
Still darker grows the shortening day;
And those who've trod the path before
Call on us now to halt no more,
But follow them wi' purpose stern –
We'll meet nae mair by Draedan burn.

We'll meet nae mair by Draedan burn –
Wi' griefs and cares our hearts are worn;
But there the stream will onward glide,
Like Time's unstaying, ceaseless glide,
And soon we'll go like those who're gone
And flowers will bloom and streams run on –
While we shall go and ne'er return,
And meet nae mair by Draedan burn!

Chirnside, August, 1855. H.
Merse Local Rhymes, No. 6.

A Song of Harvest

The flowers now fade on hill and dale,
  And faintly bees are humming;
The corn is rustling in the gale,
  And harvest days are coming:
The harping crake has left our land,
  The swallow soon will follow,
And many a merry harvest band
  Will meet on height and hollow.

A harvest hue is on the slopes,
  The wheat and oats are yellow;
And barley rigs increase our hopes
  That a' will soon be mellow:
Come a' ye lads and lassies braw,
  Get a' your sickles ready;
And blythely rank yoursels in raw,
  And ply your arms steady.

Ye bandsters come, wi' lyart pow,
  And set your sheaves in order;
Look on the fields how bright they glow,
  On baith sides o' the Border!
Pile up your stooks a' neat and clean,
  On stibble-rigs right early,
And let nae scatter'd rip be seen,
  'Mang sheaves o' ripened barley.

When corn rigs are weaving seen
  How bonny in the mornin'!
And glancin' keen are maidens' een,
  And blythesome lads are scorin'.
And when the kirn-night is come,
  They'll sing and dance fu' gladly;
And bright will be the farmer's home,
  And ne'er a ane look sadly.

Then wake the lilts o' auld lang syne,
  The sangs o' Scottish story,
The strains that tell o' *Bruce's* line,
  And *Wallace* in his glory!
And sing the ancient ballads o'er
  Of Border feud and foray,
That cheer'd our sires in days o' yore,
  And matrons auld and hoary.

And raise the strains o' later days,
  The songs are sweet and tender –
The fresh, the bright the glorious lays
  That *Burns* to earth did render;
Con a' the auld romantic rhymes
  That make our land sae cheery,
And chant them ower at harvest times, –
  Your hearts will never weary.

Soon o'er the hills o' Lammermoor
  The curtains o' the gloamin'
Will fall in crimson folds o' gore,
  And hame ye'll a' be roamin':
Then down the furrows rich wi' corn,
  Urge on your toils fu' lightly,
While joke, and sangs and rustic scorn,
  Cheer a' your reapers brightly.

The golden wheaten sheaves secure –
  The glory o' September!
But aye the sad desponding poor
  Amidst your wealth remember:
Frae your ripe fields and acres wide
  Spurn not the gleaner lowly:
Nor flout them a' wi' taunts o' pride –
  For pride is sin and folly.

Then shall the God o' Nature crown
  Your hills and vales wi' plenty;

If wealth do not on poortith frown
  Our stores will ne'er be scanty.
How glorious now in harvest day
  To view our Border grandeur!
And mid these scenes my heart will stay,
  Where'er my feet may wander.

My heart clings to the Merse's vale
  Like child unto its mother,
And O that love can never fail,
  Though a' beside should wither:
And now my chant is ended here
  While harvest scenes are glowing,
And swells my soul wi' gladsome cheer
  To see abundance flowing.

Chirnside, August 15, 1855. H.
Merse Local Rhymes, No. 7.

◇◇◇◇◇◇◇

The Auld Kirkyard of Horndean

Written on a visit to the place in 1855.

Auld Horndean, how lone a place
    For thy auld dead is here!
Thy ancient kirk is gone, alas!
    For many a long past year,
And by its ruin lie the race
    Of Border men o' weir.

Most lonely is this grassy knowe –
    At gloamin' hour how lone!
Where hemlock and dark nettles grow
    Around each mossy stone,
And mouldering mortals lie below
    Forgotten and unknown.

The auld kirk wa's are reft and bare,
    In ruin long they've lain:
And every sacred corner there
    Is open to the rain: –
But sure these ruin'd wa's declare
    To us a solemn strain.

They preach to us of sad decay,
    And o' our coming change;
They tell us all things pass away
    Within this world's wide range,
And speak o' man's short fleeting day,
    And alterations strange.

Green are the graves upon that mound,
    Green may they ever be!
Though no protection them surround,
    Of wall, of fence, of tree:
Sacred ay that spot of ground,
    Till a' the dead go free!

Since the first corpse was buried there
    Long ages hae swept drear
Across this scene of woe and care
    For a' who life do bear;
And *we* must as the pilgrims fare,
    And pilgrims vesture wear.

Some patriot hearts may here repose,
    Who in war's troubled day
Met all unblanched, their bannered foes –
    Now long they've lain in clay!
And a' their triumphs and their woes
    Are passed alike away.

Some gentle maiden, bright as morn,
    Who trode the Border side,
May lie beneath these stones – sair worn –
    Gone down oblivion's tide! –

And who might tell the wae and scorn
That on her heart did bide?

They're a' away – they've had their day –
The world's smile and frown;
And Time, like Tweed there, will not stay,
But sweeps *us* swiftly down
To the low mansions of decay,
Where all Death's sceptre own.

Few here will come the dead to mourn,
Few ponder on their fate –
How soon to dust doth man sojourn,
How short his earthly date!
O proud vain man! here take a turn,
And muse thy future state!

Mound of the dead! how *small* a spot
Compared with fields around!
But histories *large*, could they be wrote,
Might in that space be found:
They're known to One – to *us* they're not
Seen in that grassy ground.

A verdant mound, a mossy stone,
Kirkyard o' Horndean!
Is what remains o' those who're gone
Beyond this mortal scene:
And peace and silence resteth on
Thy lone, auld kirkyard green.

Chirnside, October 16, 1855. H.
Merse Local Rhymes, No. 8.

A Lament for the Bog Reeds

O lovely Nature! Blooming Queen!
Upon thy breast I'd ever lean:
For ay to me thy charms hae been
My richest treasure,
And in thy smiling look serene
There's endless pleasure.

O lead me hence to woods and dells,
Reed-shaded streams, and gushing wells,
To moorland wastes where heather-bells
Are blooming sweet;
And there, remote from Mammon's spells,
In joy we'll meet.

Take me, O take me far frae men,
Into yon deep, untrodden glen;
Or by the dank and reedy fen
I'll meet wi' thee,
And blessed beyond the worldling's ken
My heart will be.

But Nature, now thy sweet domain
By man has suffered many a strain;
And still encroaching, proud and vain,
On thy recesses,
They walk wi' Fashion's feet profane,
And scorn thy blisses.

Few spots o' this green blooming ball
To thee are left unscath'd – the thrall
Of grasping Avarice over all
Hath thrown her bane,
And fell Ambition's curse doth fall
On earth and stane.

Left to the flower, the ant, the bee
Is nae place, now, unplough'd and free,
Torn up is slope, and bank, and lea,
And ferny dean;
And scarce one bonny brae for thee
Is mossy green.

The rushy gairs, and burn-sides sweet,
They might hae left for poets' feet,
They've drain'd the bogs and mires complete;
A' knowes are torn,
Where tripp'd the hares, 'mong dewy weet,
At early morn.

And wild-wood bowers, where lovers strayd,
Or rapt hands roam'd down hazel glade,
Or sat entranc'd, deep in the shade,
They've taken away;
And our auld haunts are desolate laid
By Gain's fell sway.

Surely, the Myre they might hae spar'd
To mine, and Nature's, lov'd regard;
Its banks and holes, where sometimes lair'd
The farmer's horse,
I'd rather see, than see it wair'd
To aid Pride's course.

The grey saugh-buss, that grew lang there,
Is gane for aye – and bog-bean fair,
With a' the reedy rushy ware
That flourish'd green
In the deep vale and misty lair
O' beasts unseen.

But mostly, I lament the loss
O' tall bog-reeds that leaned across
The black moss-pits and glitty foss –
And bog-reeds slim,
That wav'd their plumes o' purple gloss
O'er well-heads dim.

Oft hae I stood, when life was new,
When hopes were bright, and cares were few,
And all was lovely in my view,
Those reeds to see.
While the braid slopes a' mellow hue
Wore to the e'e.

Those reeds a worthless crop were deem'd,
Though in my eyes they beauteous seem'd; –
And oft beside them I hae dream'd
My visions strange,
While wild Romance upon me gleam'd
Her fitful range.

The midnight breezes, sighing low,
Through those bent reeds did often go,
When silvery mists did overflow
The silent vale,
And moonbeams shed a mellow glow
O'er hill and dale.

At such an hour, lone-musing there
On long past days and friendships rare,
Sad thoughts fell on me like despair,
And passing slow
Up the steep path, wi' bosom sair,
I bore my wo.

The reeds that grew in days o' yore,
In Billy's vale we'll see no more,
Rash-buss and saugh are a' uptore,
And bog-reeds long; –
O Nature! Sure thy heart is sore
To see sic wrong!

I've lean'd on reeds as frail as thae –
They've pierc'd my hands they've been nae stay
In hours o' need – they broke away,
And let me fall,
And left me in the Mire always,
Wi' heart o' gall.

O' Nature! Sweet, benign, and grand,
To thee I give my heart, my hand –
And all thy wonders still shall stand,
Though feeble Man
May plough, and delve, and turn the land
To Lucre's plan.

By anarch Custom, sway'd and led,
In selfish Fashion's arts deep read,
And vers'd in Gain's remorseless trade,
Men thankless spurn
The bliss that Nature's freely spread
To all wha're born.

The toiling people slave and mourn
To fill Wealth's deep insatiate urn,
But few o'er Nature's glories burn
Wi' hearts sincere;
To Pride, to Gain, they all things turn,
Nor see nor hear

The beauties which around them lie,
The wonders of the earth and sky,
The voices which pass ever by
On hill and shore,
O' Nature! ope each ear and eye
To learn thy lore.

And let each longing soul be full
Of thy sweet spirit, never dull;
For me, no fate shall e'er annul
My joys in thee,
And from thee I shall ever cull
Strength, peace, and glee.

In all thy aspects, forms, and moods,
In all thy calms, convulsions, floods,
We'll trace the Power that ever broods
And rules o'er all,
And rest contented wi' thy goods,
Whate'er befall.

Chirnside, September 4, 1855. H.
Merse Local Rhymes, No. 9.

The Slaughter of Sir David Home of Wedderburn

By Ramrig and Mountfair
Came up a reiver band,
Of Southern border men,
To ravage the Merse land;
Led on by stalwart knight
The foray onward came,
To plunder, kill, and slay,
And set ilk grange on flame.

Across the Caldside moor
They pass'd in fierce array,
Our oxen, horse, and sheep,
Of a' to make a prey.
But soon the tidings flew
To Home of Wedderburn
That a band had cross'd the Tweed
That glowing summer morn.

The word flew east and west
To arm his vassals all,
And forth they came in haste
From tower, and grange, and hall;
They march'd across the plain,
Sir David led them on,
They rush'd upon the foe,
But the day they did not win.

And oh, it grieves to tell
The sad disaster then
That on Sir David fell
Amidst the battle's stour,
As forth he urg'd his power
Where spears and armour shone,
His pennon bearing on
Through troops of Southern men.

Borne backward in the fray,
Grasping a splintered lance,
The knight was wounded sore,
Where swords around did glance;
And there by Towie's well
The border chieftain fell,
And wounded there he lay
Bleeding to death away,
Down in the grassy dale,
While o'er his visage pale
The cold and clammy dew
Of life's last struggle drew.

Wi mournfu' dirge and wail
They bore his corpse away,
Along by Swinton tower,
While gloamin's shadows grey
Sunk over hall and bower.

Upon the western slope
Of Folley-hills still shone
The beams of parting day,
While in the valley lone
The slaughtered vassals lay;
And groans of dying men
Through all the silent night
Were heard across the plain,
Beneath the starry light.

The grief and agony,
The sorrow and the pain,
Which fell that dreary night
Upon the field of slain,
Have long forgotten been,
And in Oblivion's main
Those warriors names hae sunk
Never to rise again.

The ploughmen o' the Merse
Hae plough'd their dust aboon,
And never once have thought
O' that bloody afternoon,
When the knight o' Wedderburn
By Towie's hamlet fell;
Where long there stood a cross
The mournfu' deed to tell.

But broken is the cross,
And down to darkness gone
The feats of martial fame
That our Border fathers won;
And on the Merse are rank'd
Home's shimmering spears no more,
Though still we love to sing
Their gallant deeds of yore;

When through the mist of years
Their warlike train is seen,
Their pennons and their spears,
And war steeds prancing keen;
We burn with ardour then,
And sing their glories o'er,
And love the ballads well
Of ancient border lore.

Chirnside, November 24, 1855. H.
Merse Local Rhymes, No. 10.

Note: The event recorded in the above lines occurred in July, 1524, at a place called Towie, which lay betwixt the village of Ramrig and Swinton. A cross was erected on the spot in commemoration of the fatal affray – but it has long since disappeared, and there is no place now bearing the name of Towie.

The Wandering Widow's Lament

The following verses were written on seeing a poor, pale, forlorn-looking and emaciated woman sitting shivering by the wayside, with three helpless children, the eldest not above eight years of age. It was a chilly and moist autumnal evening, and she had kindled a fire by the side of a brook, called the Kebbyburn, near Hutton Hall, and there she intended to pass the night with her infant charge. The poor creature seemed in the last stages of consumption, and I entreated her to seek the shelter of the neighbouring farmer's barn or shed. But she replied that "she did not like to be troublesome to anybody, and she would rather lie under the hedge, as it mattered little where she lodged for the short time she had to stay on earth, and she hoped soon to meet with him who had gone before her. And as for her wee bairnies – naming each of them – she was forced to leave them to Providence, who would take care of them." Her heart was full, and she could say no more, and I was necessitated to leave her. This was in the autumn of 1854, and what afterwards became of her and the poor children I never could learn.

The yellow leaves fa' aff the trees,
The yellow leaves fa' fast, Johnnie;
The drizzling rain comes chilly down
And cauld's the northern blast, Johnnie.
Like forest leaves my powers decay,
My days are waning fast away,
And here I can nae langer stay –
Oh, I maun part wi' thee, Johnnie.

Thy feet are bare, thy face is pale,
Ye waesome look at me, Johnnie;
Oh, wha will kiss that bonny face
When I'm away frae thee, Johnnie?
Oh, wha will hap thee frae the cauld?
Wha will thee in their arms enfauld?
For I've nae hame, nae house, nor hauld,
Where I can shelter gie, Johnnie.

And Mary, there, sae sweet and fair,
Sic sorrow's in her e'e, Johnnie;
And, shivering pale beneath the gale,
I'm wae her waes to see, Johnnie.
Some sheltered spot might save us still,
And make us bear this world's ill,
And help us up life's weary hill;
But hopes o' that are vain, Johnnie.

And Nanny, too, my best beloved! –
How can I part wi' thee, Nanny?
Wi' dreary care my heart is sair,
My heart is sair for thee, Nanny.
Oh, soon, within the cauld cauld grave,
The rank green grass will owre me wave,
And wild the winter winds will rave
My wasted form aboon, Nannie!

Where will ye wander, bairnies mine,
When I am cauld in clay, Johnnie?
Oh, could I take ye a' wi' me,
To sleep out night and day, Johnnie!
For, oh, I fear your lot, like mine,
In this cauld world will be to pine;
And Fortune on ye ne'er will shine –
Nae friends to help ye here, Johnnie!

Your faither's gane, and sair I maen,
And miss him frae our head, Johnnie!
He'll come nae mare to sooth our care,
Or help us in our need, Johnnie.
Now ilka day I lang to rest
This weary, sair, distracted breast
Beside your faither – surely blest –
Sae gude and gentle ay, Johnnie!

Poor helpless things! sad is your fate!
    My sair heart clings to thee, Johnnie.
But soon – oh, soon I'll frae you part,
    Then what you'll hae to dree, Johnnie
The leaves are scatter'd by the blast:
Into their graves, like me, they haste.
My troubled days are now near past,
    And sair I grieve for thee, Johnnie.

Though want and woe may overflow
    Your hapless days a' here, Johnnie,
We'll meet again where there's nae rain,
    Nor cruel folk to fear, Johnnie.
I'll keep my arms around ye a'
As lang's I hae a breath to draw;
And soon I'll be where rain or snaw
    Will never grieve us mair, Johnnie.

Creep closer – closer to my side;
    I'll hap thee frae the cauld, Mary,
Your shoon are torn, your heart's forlorn,
    You're sair wi' travel gall'd, Mary.
Nae mortal kens the waes ye dree;
But ane aboon your sorrows see,
And he'll a hame and shelter gie
    To waefu', wandering bairns, Mary!

The morn will come to gladden some:
    It will not gladden me, Nanny!
Ye'll sleep beneath the chilling sky,
    While tears drap frae my e'e, Nannie.
The morn will come – but I'll be gane;
The morn will come – but I'll be taen,
And this poor heart be cauld's a stane
    Ye'll waken me nae mair, Nannie!

Dear Johnnie, man, ye'll miss me sair!
        Oh mammy's name ye'll ca', Johnnie,
But ca' in vain – oh, mournfu' thought!
        It tears my heart in twa, Johnnie.
Oh Nannie, Mary, Johnnie sweet,
When will we a' thegither meet,
And rest our weary wandering feet,
        And never part again, Johnnie?

I ance had hopes to see you up,
        Your mother's waes to cheer, Johnnie;
But that sweet drap into my cup
        To me's no given here, Johnnie.
But cling together, bairnies a',
When I frae you am forc'd awa';
And though the tempest on ye blaw,
        Still mind your mother dear, Johnnie!

Chirnside, October 25, 1855. H.
Merse Local Rhymes, No. 11.

Simprin Kirk

Written on a recent visit to the ruins of Simprin Church.

Where sages o'er the earth have trode,
Where poets held their calm abode,
And holy men conversed with God –
Such places still
Are sacred deem'd in soil and sod,
On vale and hill.

Hence Simprin to my heart hath been
A sacred consecrated scene,
Since in life's early morn serene
My mother dear
Told how that Boston preached keen
There many a year.

She praised his Works – a matchless pearl –
His manse she'd seen, when but a girl,
Ere ruin did its roof tree tirl,
And bared its wa'
And held that time wad never swirl
His fame awa'.

Yes Simprin still shall woven be
With Boston's name eternally
Where down i' th' Merse he preached free
In her auld kirk,
And shed the light o' Gospel day
Midst sin's thick mirk.[1]

Affectionate, sincere and kind,
With earnest heart and zealous mind,
A faithful watcher of the blind,
There Boston pray'd,
And there to husbandman and hind,
The truth display'd.

He grasp'd the banner of the cross;
All earth to him was dust and dross,
And everything "he counted loss"
For Christ the Lord,
And urg'd on all to follow close
Th' eternal word.

His little flock around him press'd
With glowing and delighted breast
As urging them to seek their rest
In Heaven's domain,
Where all the sanctified and blessed
With Christ shall reign.

The glories of the Heavenly state,
The terrors of the Judgment seat,
He held to view – and bade them wait
With steadfast faith,
Until they saw unfold the gate
Of life and death.

He show'd how poor the pomps of earth,
The vanities of mortal birth,
The false and fleeting joys of earth –
How far from peace!
And said that there was nothing worth
But Faith and Grace.

All earthly pleasures are but dust
The gold is dim, the silver rust –
And he in wealth who puts his trust
To woe shall fall;
The power of man, to joys of lust,
Shall perish all!

And here within these ruin'd walls,
Where rain and snow now freely falls,
Was sounded forth the "Gospel calls",
By Boston leal,
In times when truth had many thralls
And woes to feel.

He stood and watched in godly fear
Upon this watch tower, sleeping ne'er,
But firm in faith from year to year
'Gainst sin he fought,
And all the powers that men could rear
Could turn him not.

He pointed to the sinner's doom,
In hell's perpetual lurid gloom;
He warn'd "to fly from wrath to come"
With earnest soul –
For in Christ's love for all was room,
While time should roll.

Within that roofless, narrow bound,
'Tis surely sacred, hallowed ground,
Since Boston here of old was found
Christ's cause to plead;
And here he walked the grave yard round
With solemn tread.

'Mong pastors of the olden day
Who held o'er Simprin kirk their sway,
The honour'd dust they here did lay
Of Boston's sire,[2]
Where till the last loud trumpet's bray
'Twill rest entire.

And hid within this narrow fold,
Some praying simple men of old,
Who heard "the Gospel scheme" unroll'd
By Boston's lips,
Here mingle silent in the mould,
In death's eclipse.

My fancy hovers o'er the scene
Where the old Border men have been, –
The stern in soul, the patriot keen,
There calmly sleep,
With maidens in their time serene,
No more to weep.

And in that lovely, green kirkyard
They rest beneath the grassy sward –
The fathers who our land did guard,
Long since forgot; –
So Simprin, thee I'll aye regard
A hallowed spot.

Chrinside, January 12, 1856. H.
Merse Local Rhymes, No. 12.

[1] *It is said that the people of the Merse, even in Boston's time, were very wild and irreligious. In homely elegy on Boston's death, he is represented as "a rose upon a thorn", blooming, as it were, amidst a brake of brambles and thorns.*

[2] *John Boston, who was from Ayrshire, and the father of the Rev. Thomas Boston, was interred in the burial place of the ministers of Simprin.*

The Battle of Halidon Hill

"On Saint Margetey's eve, as I vow tell
Befelle the victory of Halidoune hill
In the year of God Almighty
A m.iiic and iii, and thirty
There this bateill befelle,
At Berwick beside the towne." – Minot

AWAY, all away, in a dreadful array,
Ere the close of the day they had fled from the fray
Away, away by the Galloping Green;
The Douglas is down in a deadly swoon,
In the midst o' the strife he has parted wi' life,
In the front o' the battle no more to be seen.

Wi lances broke in the battle's shock,
Wi' banners torn and hearts forlorn,
They are pressing away to the north countrie;
Wounded and sore, and streak'd wi' gore,
In sad dismay, ere the battle is o'er,
They are wandering away wi' their chivalrie.

Wi' shout on shout, in the dreadful rout,
Where foe meets foe there is ruin and woe,
They stagger and reel in the tumult sore,
In a crimson flood o' the warriors's blood,
The slain sink down in the gory mud,
And the battle's stour the field sweeps o'er.

Ghastly and pale – they fail! they fail!
In the deadly stound on the battle ground,
The brave are sunk to their endless sleep;
The day is lost: and our broken host,
Are quailing before the triumph and boast
O' their tyrant foes, as they onward sweep.

O' woe! oh woe! – the southern foe
Pressed sair that day on our broken array,
That eagerly bent to the hills o' the west,
They leave on the plain the wounded and slain,
And the day closes sad on their anguish and pain,
While thousands hae sunk to their dreamless rest.

The trampling steed, in his foaming speed,
They will fear no more – they will fear no more!
They hae reach'd the goal beyond life's ills;
In the clay laid low they will dread no foe,
Nor heed they now either thrust or blow,
Nor yearn to get back to their country's hills.

The dew comes down silent and dull
On the dead men strew'd on the brow o' the hill;
In heaps and ranks they lie ghastly pale!
Oh woe! oh woe! for that overthrow,
They hae fled, they hae fled, and the brave lie low,
And in ha' and cot there is weeping and wail.

Away! – and away by Foulden away,
They are trooping past in the gloomin' grey –
Behind they are leaving the field o' the slain
The shrieks and granes o' the dying ones
Are echoing sad over Halidon Hill,
While the vanquished host passes over the plain.

By Douglas-dike, where the Douglas fell,
We hae stood gaz'd over hill and dell,
And the Tweed's fair river flowing free;
On the town and bay that stretch away,
And the Cheviot's border mountain heigh.

On that steep ascent wi' the barley blent,
Wi' their glittering spears in the long past years,
The Scotchmen press'd to the martial fray,
But drench'd wi' their gore ere the day was o'er,
The daisies droop'd and the brave no more
Could wield the sword, or the battle stay.

They are gone! – they are gone, every hero's bone
Is moulded to dust upon Halidon,
Where dim'd was the glory o' Bannockburn;
But the flag o' peace now floats along
The hills and vales o' this land o' song
And that strife of old no more we'll moan.

Chrinside, February 16, 1856. H.
Merse Local Rhymes, No. 13.

◇◇◇◇◇◇◇

Moorland Joy

"Many a loved and lovely scene,
Which I no more may visit; are ye not
Thus still my own?" – Bernard Barton

O were ye ever at Kilpalet?
Drank ye ever o' its burn?
Did you ever roam the moorlands,
On a lovely harvest morn?
When the wild bee there was humming
Ower the heather's purple bloom –
Sat you then by yon grey cairn,
Some old hero's lonely tomb?

Did you hear the wild bee humming
Ower the mossy banks and braes?
Did you see the rash-bush waving
In the noon tide's sultry haze?
Heard you – far upon the mountain,
Bleating to the shepherd's cry,
Flocks o' moor-bred ewes and lambkins,
While the cloud shades hastened by?

Did you sit beside the fountain,
Far away among the heather?
Did you listen to its murmurs,
While its mosses green you'd gather?
Did you hear the gentle breezes
Moaning through the hair-grass tall?
And mark the mist wreaths on the mountain
When the day was near the fall?

Did you hear the wild bee hameward
Hasten to its mossy cell?
Did not then the soul o' freedom
In your bosom burn and swell?
Lonely roaming through the moorlands
Ower the heath-clad Lammermoor,
Did not joy unbounded fill you,
Far remote from fashion's power?

Patriot feet hae wandered freely
By those mountain passes green:
In the days o' Bruce and Wallace,
There the hero's march hath been!
Still to yonder wastes o' heather
Turns my heart wi' longing sair,
And still beside Kilpalet's burnie
I would roam for ever mair!

Or South to Dirrington I'd wander,
Where my fathers watch'd their ewes,
And climb the law's old scalp sae hoary,

And owre the wild scene sit and muse:
Roaming a' the moorland over,
Sweet's the freedom – ever sweet;
Sweet 'mong heather-bells to wander,
Where in burns I'd lave my feet!

There the shepherd's wi' their hirsels,
In the ages long gone by,
Roam'd the wide and trackless moorlands,
Neath a' changes of the sky;
They had hopes and fears as we have,
They had toils to undergo: –
All their fears and hopes are ever,
All their joys and all their wo.

Sweet to roam the hills o' heather,
Seeking flowers and berries blae,
Drinking frae the joys o' nature,
When bright glows the harvest day!
Sweet's the fragrance o' the moorlands,
Sweet the sounds and voices there!
Mild the breezes sweep the moorlands –
Soothing to the soul o' care!

Sweet among the knowes and brakens
Sing the lintics, chanting clear;
Sweet among the bogs and mosses
Flora's gems the loneness cheer;
Sweet in nature in the moorlands,
All her shows and sounds are sweet;
The ceaseless hum that fills the moorlands,
Makes the lone heart gladly beat!

April 19, 1856. H.
Merse Local Rhymes, No. 14.

The Braes o' the Eye

Air – "Tweedside"

How sweet are the braes o' the Eye,
How green are its forests and fair,
That wave on yon slopes smiling high,
Below the old hills that are bare!
In the deans that are lonesome and deep,
Where the fern plumes droop owre the well;
How sweet to recline 'neath the steep,
And muse in the green shady dell.

How sweetly we've pass'd the long day,
In the Brockhole's dean strolling along,
Where the flowers bloom sae sweet on the brae,
And the happy birds carol their song,
How bless'd in the woods were the hours,
That we spent 'neath the fair blooming tree,
And sweet were the green hazel bowers,
That hung o'er my Nancy and me.

The rowan-tree bloom'd on the brae,
The rose in its beauty was there,
The birds in the brake o' the slae,
Rejoiced in that season sae fair;
The burn stole by wi' its song
The bonny sweet flowers by its side,
And gladness – their blossoms among,
Fill'd our hearts wi' a full-flowing tide!

How sweet are the banks o' the Eye,
Where down by Shawbraes and the Mill,
The fresh days o' youth gilded bye,
And joy through my bosom did thrill.
The alder-bowered water is dear
Where we bathed in the clear flowing stream
Where the flowers in their glory appear,
And rejoice in ilk sweet summer gleam.

The sweetest hours spent in life's span,
Are spent in some wood's mossy dell;
While the leave's o' our life are not wan,
And peace in our bosom doth dwell,
Then let me go forth to the groves,
'Ere the yellow leaves strew the green sod,
And there we'll recall a' our loves,
That hae gilded our grief-chequer'd road.

Through each tangled glade let us rake,
Frae Renton to Houndwood a' down;
And we'll roam ilka dell and green brake,
While the waters send forth a sweet croon;
The birds and the bees as we go,
Will banish ilk sorrowful sigh;
And the flowers in their beauty that blow,
Will soothe our lone hearts on the Eye.

Chirnside, April 19, 1856. H
Merse Local Rhymes, No. 15.

The Chapel Haugh

By the side of the Whitadder a little below Ninewells, but on the opposite side of the water, lies a small piece of ground, belonging to the farm of Stuart's Law, and on the lands of Allanbank, which is called the Chapel Haugh: so called because a chapel once existed near the place in remote times. It was on this haugh that the great conventicle was held, in the year 1671 – which is usually called "the great communion of East Nisbet – three thousand two hundred persons having communicated there on that occasion".

The water glides softly away, away
Down by the bonny chapel haugh brae,
Where many good folk o' the auld langsyne
Partook o' the holy bread and wine.
They sat on the grass by the river clear,
When the barley hung down its ripening ear,
And the breezes softly waved the corn
Owre the yellow rigs i' the harvest morn,
And sunny and warm the day wore by,
Under the clear blue autumn sky,
And white-headed callants and auld beards gray,
Sat on the bonny Chapel haugh brae;
And sweet smiling maidens like daisies red,
Sat there entranc'd wi' a holy dread;
And matrons auld, runkled and sear,
Sucked in the Word wi' a pleasing fear;
And many a blue-bannet was lifted there.
When the men o' God arose to prayer
There were Dickson and Welch, and Riddel and Rae,
And Blackadder too, frae Troquair in the west
One of the boldest, and one of the best –
A' preachin' wi' pith by the Chapel haugh brae,
Outpouring their hearts without halt or rest,
To the bold Covenanters, stern and stout
That gather'd from the country a' round about.
O sic an assembly was ne'er before seen
A' sat a' sae douce on the Chapel haugh green,
On that glorious August day serene!
Their singing sweet gaed floating away

O'er the fields 'boon the Chapel haugh brae,
And the herd boy sitting afar wi' his kye
Was melted to tears wi' the melody:
And the old Roman camps now waving in grain
Never heard sic a plaintive and holy strain,
Through a' the lang ages o' time's fleeting tide
Since the Roman stood by the Whitadder side[1]
And look'd the green banks o' Ninewells o'er,
And thought of his own sweet Italian shore,
On the haugh and the brae by the Whitadder side,
That great assembly couldna abide,
And they a' are gone from the haugh and the brae
To walk in the light of eternal day.
But hallowed for aye will be the scene,
Where our bauld forbears on the turf did lean,
And worshipp'd wi' hearts devoted, sincere,
By the Whitadder side their Saviour dear;
That spot should be sacred for evermore,
Since on that harvest day it bore,
True patriot men o' the times of yore;
Who rather to death would hunted be
Than bend to kings a servile knee –
Kings, who fetters and chains wad bind
On mountain men o' the free born mind
And the Scots true loyal men will be
If their conscience is not tamper'd wi';
But they'll never yield to lord or king,
Their creed or worship in any thing;
So in our heart we'll aye revere,
The men o' the Merse who worshipp'd here;
For sacred rights who fought and bled –
For rights by which we're now made glad,
And these rights we'll hold wi' jealous care,
While breathing God's free blessed air.
And oft we've sat by the water cool,
While the sun shone hot on stream and pool
Alone, half slumbering 'midst fragrant flowers,
In calm repose at the noon's bright hours,
And thought we heard the martyr's psalm,

In choral sweetness, filling the calm,
From a multitude vast of worshippers there
Bursting from hearts sore tired wi' care, –
That great solemnity's over and gone
And the song of the Martyrs is still as the stone –
The water is lapping away by the green,
And the Martyrs there no more will be seen,
To sing and preach, to preach and pray,
Down by the bonny Chapel-haugh brae!
But to our hearts will aye be dear,
That haugh and brae by the water clear,
Where was held the feast o' the Martyrs good
In times long past – at the risk o' blood.

June 14, 1856. H
Merse Local Rhymes, No. 16.

[1] *A Roman camp, now ploughed over, once existed in the immediate neighbourhood of the Chapel haugh.*

◇◇◇◇◇◇◇◇

Fast Castle

Thou hast heard the captive's moan,
When the ocean raging wild,
Broke upon the barrier stone,
And the rugged rocks up-piled,
Where yon sea-bird sitteth lone,
Like a hermit self exiled.

Oft thy hoary time worn cliffs
Have borne the shock of war;
And thou hast seen King Edward's skiffs
Sail southward from Dunbar,
Freighted with cowed, defeated chiefs
From Bannock's battle far.

The old grey tower, and sea-ward peak
    Have oft been lost and won;
While deep below in rocky creek
    The billows still clash on;
And foaming at thy foot they break,
    As wont in ages gone,
When border feuds did often streak
    Our banks and braes wi' gore,
And oft was paled the martial cheek
    Thy port-cullis before.

Thy crusted towers or rifted wall,
    Long looking to the sea,
Past ages to our minds recall –
    Ages no more to be –
When stern old warriors trode thy hall,
    Or battled on the lea.

In centuries past, remote and dim,
    A monarch's couch thou'st been;
And from the south in gallant trim,
    Fair Margaret, the Queen,
Up to thy barbican did climb
    To gaze on ocean scene,
On Bass, and May, and Lothian's shore,
    And hills and islets green,
And frith and bay that gladsome bore
    The gloamin' tinge serene.

Wild, on the ledge of ocean wide,
    Thy ruins there remain;
And the rude rocks laved by the tide,
    Or wash'd by wintery rain,
Still in their rugged forms abide
    Whilst thou away dost wane.
On the green downs that skirt the shore,
    Blooms sweet the blue hare-bell,
And mountain violets spread their store
    Fair by yon rocky dell;

And there they bloom'd in days before
  Fast Castle's ramparts fell;
And fresh and young they'll flourish still,
While ocean's billows swell,
And sunbeams on the heathy hill
  Of Nature's glories tell.

The mist comes o'er the troubled sea,
  And shrouds the headlands all,
And Dowlaw dean and Lumsden shore,
  Are covered with its pall,
And o'er the moorland upland lea,
  Is heard the sea-bird's call,
That seems to mourn time's changes o'er
  Fast Castle's ruined wall.

A dreary desolate abode
  Down by the restless main
Where dark brow'd Logan often trode,
  And dreed the traitors pain,
When tempests o'er the ocean rode,
  Driving the sleet and rain.

He was the last o' Logan's race
  Who held that sea-wash'd tower,
And fallen from his pride of place,
  And reft of lands and power,
His name was blackened with disgrace,
  That stains it to this hour.

What has been here of woe and wail,
  Of mirth and revelry,
No man of earth can tell the tale
  The peril or the glee,
That here has past with breeze and gale
  Since first this castle hie,
Was built upon the beetling rock
  Close by the sleepless sea;
And how in war's tumultuous shock,

Its gate the siege did quell
And fruitless on its rampart broke
The Southern's prowess snell;
Though sometimes underneath their stroke
This feudal fortress fell.

And this is all! a lonesome site,
A shatter'd mouldering pile –
A ruin grey, on which alight
The birds of rock and isle,
And where the winds of ocean fight,
In raving, solemn style,
And tempests howl in furious might,
And ocean's billows boil;
And through the dark and dismal night
Pass fearful sounds of dread,
Like shrieking ghosts in dire affright,
Or seamen hard bested,
While gleaming fitful on the sight
The beacon glances red.

And this is all, Fast Castle now,
All that remains of thee!
And sitting on the rock's green brow
And looking on the sea,
While crested billows shoreward flow,
I musing thoughtfully,
See visions of old-times forth-grow
From clouds and mists that flee,
O'er the dark brow of wild St Abbs,
Or over Lumsden lea;
Or when the veil of gloamin' robes
St Helen's fallen fane,
I cross the moor and broomy stobs,
And dream past days again;
While dies the wind on Redheugh shore,
And quiet lulls the main,
And labour's at Auld Cambus o'er,
And night bedews the plain.

I leave behind the ruin'd hold,
Fast Castle's rifted steep,
And slowly o'er the heathy wold
My homeward way I keep;
And soon the ancient bowers behold
That circle Houndwood deep
With shade on shade – a forest old
Where once the deer did sleep;
And down the hill, and o'er the Eye
I pass with weary feet.

I reach my home while the red moon
Wheels upward from the sea;
And slumber o'er me presses soon,
And wraps me soothingly,
While dreams of war in awful stoun'
Pass on my tranced ee;
And warriors march to battle boun',
In glittering panoply;
And armed walls and towers are seen
With banners waving free!

And rushing hosts, and foaming steeds
Both monks and nuns appear;
And martial Abbot onward leads
His bands with bow and spear
And forth from Coldingham proceeds
The monks with warlike gear;
And rout, and rally, and defeat,
And tumult and dismay,
Fill my night visions – soon to fleet
Like morning mists away.

July 5, 1856. H.
Merse Local Rhymes, No. 17.

Childhood

There's nae joy in this world, wi' the joy can compare
That blessed wee bairns who hae freedom to stare;
Who healthy and clean roam free from ilka morn
To pluck the bright flowers which the waysides adorn.

Unrestricted and happy, free, to wander at will,
By silent green lanes, mossy banks, or clear rill:
O wha wad their mirth and their gladness restrain,
Or frown on their pastimes wi' cauldrife disdain?

We wad keep a' the bairns frae the toil and the strife
And let them never ken o' the troubles o' life;
Let them frolic and play 'mang the lang yellow broom,
And wander away where the wild roses bloom.

The moor and the meadow, the wood and the dell,
Are places befitting bairnhood well:
In the free open air, let them wander aye free,
Where the merle sings sweet, in the green forest tree.

The laverocks rejoice ower the fresh dewy sod,
Where the gowan lifts up its wee face to our God,
And the peesweep and partridge ower the furrows delight
To lead forth their broods in the dawning's first light.

By the green shooting corn and the clover ridge sweet
When the craiks harp unceasing, in their summer's retreat,
There wander ye bairns and listen the song,
The sounds and the voices that to nature belong.

O keep them not pent up in schools fetid halls,
When fresh ower the green earth, the summer rain falls:
Wi' book, and wi' questions, o' dinnae them tease
For the teachings o' Nature are better than these.

'Mong the beauties and wonders surrounding us here
'Tis much they will learn to illume their career
By our hearts ever dear is the learning we get
When bairnies we roam – as we ne'er can forget

Where the low creeping brambles the hedges en-twine
When the moth and the beetle enjoy the sunshine,
It rejoices out heart happy children to meet
Plucking posies of wild flowers, around their wee feet.

Where the fountain wells out, 'neath the green sunny brae,
Let them roll on the moor a' the lang sunny days,
Let them chase the wild bee ower bank, knowe and cairn
Or bide wi' the rabbit among the lang fern.

On the blackberry bank, where the bonny blue bells
Wave in summer's saft wind 'yont the brown heathy fells,
And the sweet purple bloom of the thyme's fragrant flowers
Embalms wi' their beauty the shepherd track'd moors.

Let the bairns gang there in their rambling free,
Afar frae the troubles o' Man's destinie;
Where bullreeds and rushes o'er the burn's course bloom
And the lang meadow queen waves its snowy white plume.

There sit ye my bairnies afar frae the town
And wear the rush belt, green helmet and crown;
Though the favour and wealth o' this warld ye may gain,
Ye'll ne'er be sae happy, tho ye'd ca't a' your ain.

Ye may lead the bright train o' Fashion's gay core,
Or in paths of renown, march forth wi' your store,
But ye'll ne'er be sae happy, whatever betide,
As when pleting the rushes on yon burn side.

Grasp ye at riches, possessions, and power,
They'll soon become ashes, what'er be your dower,
Bind ye the sheaves o' the barley or wheat
But toiling and sorrow ye surely shall meet.

Care comes wi' age – and life's pomps they are vain,
And ye ne'er will come back to your childhood again;
The sweet time o' bairnhood's passing away,
And soon – O too soon! – its joys maun decay.

Where blue curly-doddys bloom bright on the knowes,
And the burn through the flags, in its loneliness rowes,
O there – never there will your haunts be again
But toss'd unreposing on life's stormy main.

Ye'll lang to return to the scenes o' your prime,
And sit on the braes perfum'd wi' the thyme,
Where the happy wild bee, booms gloriously by,
And the lang tufts o' hair grass i' the saft breezes sigh.

In the wood where the hazel and roses entwine,
Nae mair will ye wander at day's calm decline –
Frae lone mossy haunts ye've departed for aye,
For the joy o' our bairn-time hae but a short stay.

But happy – still happy may childhood aye run,
In green mossy places, illumed by the sun;
Our homes wad be cheerless, our cots a' forlorn,
Were our bairns away, never more to return.

The bairns! The bairns keep our hearts ever green,
They're the gems o' the world on which our hopes lean; –
Then, O keep them free frae the toil and the strife,
And the troubles that darken the *Manhood* o' life!

Chirnside, July 16, 1856. H.
Merse Local Rhymes, No. 18.

On the Decease of an Old Husbandman who Died on the Eve of Harvest

Like a shock o' mellow wheat,
He the welcome grave did meet,
And he sleeps in silence now,
Wi' the turf upon his brow;
We'll ne'er meet wi' him again,
By the plots o' bending grain.

Sixty harvests hast thou shorn
In the fields the mellow corn;
'Mong the stooks o' barley rough,
Thou hast oft had toil aneuch;
Barley fields o' ripening hue,
Aye were glorious in they view;
And though harvest toils are sair,
Thou rejoiced in these to share.

Down the stubble ridges sere,
Oft we heard thee chanting clear,
Some old stave of Border song,
Striding sturdily along,
While the plaintive simple swell
Echoed far o'er bank and dell.
Kempin' in the sultry day
Muckle strength thou did display
'Mong the rustling bearded bere
Fast thou piled thy sickle clear,
And thou would'st not then be beat,
Sweltering in September heat.
In the shady hedge at noon
Gladly sat ye wi' the boon,
Where the nut-brown yill was sweet,
To allay the harvest heat;
Often there in fun and glee,
Wi' the lave you held the spree,
Rowin' o'er the clover green,
Towzlin' wi' the lassies keen,

Round the stooks or by the dike,
Sportin' like a shepherd's tyke!
But the oats or barley mair,
Ne'er will bend before you there,
And the sheaves o' golden wheat
You'll bindna in the harvest heat;
A' your harvest toils are done,
And your useful course is run,
And your sickle by is laid,
Rust is gathering on its blade,
And na mair you'll shear the corn,
In the dewy harvest morn,
Or pile the full sheaves, winnowed well,
On the stack wi' muckle skill.

Age was on thee! Poortith too;
Had the world more need of you? –
Weary on the road of life,
Thou hast left its toil and strife,
Thou hast laid thy burdens down,
Where thou fears't no tyrant's frown, –
Silent creep you to your rest;
Soft repose for age is best;
Thon hast borne the battle's stour,
Life's long battle, hard and dour;
Lie you down in yonder shade,
Death for thee a bed hath made.

In the strife o' mortal men;
Thou nae bitterness will ken;
Sore on thee life's tempest blew,
And thy days o' ease were few;
But it's past – and ne'er again
Shalt thou bear its bitter rain;
Winter, wi' its keenest blast
O'er thy grave its snaw will cast,
But you'll never feel its frost,
When it drives its withering host
O'er the hills and valleys fierce;

Cold will ne'er thy dwelling pierce.
When the breeze o' Spring shall sigh,
Thou beneath its breath shalt lie
Calm and silent as the stone
That beside thy grave is shown;
Trees may bud and grass may grow,
Thou their verdure shalt not know;
Summer will the roses bring,
And the lark and mavis sing,
But thou shalt not hear nor see
Bloom or floweret, bird or bee.

O'er the Merse and Lammermoor
Corn will wave in sun and shower;
When the fields a' yellow lie
In the harvest's beaming eye,
Reapers hearty, clean and trig
Shear again the loaden rig;
But thou wilt not meet them then,
Where the rural maidens fain,
Toil wi' glee among the corn
And their toils are blithely borne;
Ne'er again thy witty saws
Shall arouse their loud guffaws;
Ne'er again thy sage address
Will their wanton mirth repress.

When the Harvest feast is spread,
And the rustics a' are glad,
And the merry dancers ply
Underneath the autumn sky,
And the youngsters 'mang the stacks,
Spend the night in fun and cracks;
While the white mist calm and slow,
Creeps o'er hollows far below;
And the moon o'er stook and tree
Sheds her glory o'er the lea –
Thou shalt never more be there,
In the kirn joy.s to share;

Thou shalt never more repine
That thou can'st not dance, or shine
In the band, at the kirn,
Or for feasts or revels yearn: –
Through the downward ages slow,
Thou shalt sleep the grass below;
Sweeping o'er thy mouldering clay,
Oft shall pass the harvest day;
There thou still shall sleeping be,
While the breezes stir the sea,
And the breath o' harvest morn,
Gently waves the ripening corn,
Wi' thy partner on life's scene,
Thou shalt ever sleep serene, –
Active virtues, tiring never,
Made her aye a frugal liver;
Rural labour's country pleasures,
Were to her the dearest treasures,
And now she's left life's troublous day,
To be laid in kindred clay,
Wi' her bairns a' sleeping near,
Where there's not a sigh or tear.

Sleep my brother! take thy rest –
Thou had'st aye a tranquil breast;
Gentle soul and heart were thine,
Though thy lot had little shine;
Sorrow now will wring thee not,
Wealth will scowl na at thy lot;
Pride no more will come thee nigh,
Fools no more will make thee sigh,
Sons o' Mammon, set on earth,
Ne'er will scare thee wi' their mirth;
Slander's voice thou shalt not hear,
Evil tongues thou shalt not fear;
Gain, and lies, and treachery,
Shall be banish'd far from thee;
And the oppressor's direful tread
Never more will crush thy head;

Pain, and strife, and weariness
Ne'er will now invade thy bless;
A' thy troubles now shall cease,
Thou shalt rest in "perfect peace".
Wi' thy kinsfolk, langsyne dead,
Thou shall rest thy weary head;
Waving o'er thee, ages there,
Kirk-yard grass will shade thy lair,
And the bee-lov'd clover white
O'er thee bloom in sweet delight.

August 18, 1856. H.
Merse Local Rhymes, No. 19.

◇◇◇◇◇◇◇◇

The Bughts o' Choicelea: A Pastoral Song

The picture here exhibited refers to a period 80 or 100 years preceding the present.

"There's as good cheese in Choicelea,
As ever was chew'd wi' chafts."
Old Rhyme

There's pastoral braes at Choicelea town,
Where runs yon burn down clearly,
And to the bughts the maids are boun',
Sweet liltin' a' fu' cheer'ly;
They milk the ewes at e'en and morn,
While sweet by th' moorlands singin',
The birdies chant aboon the corn,
And the air wi' joy is ringin'.

The shepherds at the early dawin',
Lead frae the faulds their hirsels bonny,
That they may feed on hained lawin',
And crop the clover beds fu' mony.

'Tis sweet when mornin' mist and haze
Yet round the bowers o' Langton gather,
To weet your feet on Choicelea braes,
Or roam away among the heather.

And sweet it is, at milking hours,
To meet at bughts the lassies cheery;
And hear frae yon the hawthorn bowers,
The laugh and song o' shepherds merry;
'Tis sweet, frae many udders full,
To see the skails and cogs o'erflowing
Wi' milkness rich – while up the hill,
The let-out ewes are freely going.

At curds and whey, they're ever thrang,
At Choicelea town they're working ever,
Yearning and churning a' day lang.
Or making tubs and bowies clever;
And ye wad say it's a sicht to praise
To see my Ann gang kilted, scourin' –
The light and joy o' Choicelea braes,
Her bonny smile on a' things showerin'.

In milk and whey and cheese unmatch'd,
Auld Choicelea will remain for ever;
As clean, and sweet, and a' unblashed,
And pure as ony mountain river:
Unmatch'd the cheese o' Choicelea braes,
Her bonny ewes gang a' together:
And lilting there the queen o' Raes
Comes linkin' down among the heather!

September, 1856. H.
Merse Local Rhymes, No. 20.

"Note – As the health of the writer of these Rhymes has been, for sometime past, in a precarious state, this will likely be the last of the series that will appear in these columns."
Berwick Advertiser, *November 15, 1856.*

Other Poems

The Return Home

To Lothian land I bade farewell,
   Up Danskein path I slowly trode,
And hailed with joy the heathy fell
   That lay around my homeward road.

Down Fasney Water's rugged side
   The fleecy mists yet lingering lay,
And far across the moorland wide
   Round shepherds wheel'd the lapwing grey.

The moss appeared in greener hue,
   And by the burn were fresher seen
Soft piles of grass with pearls o' dew,
   And budding briers were in the dean.

The gowan's rosy tips were gem'd
   With dew-drops of the April morn,
And while the mist the mountains seam'd,
   I lonesome pass'd Kilpalet burn.

The ploughman whistled o'er the lea,
   And gladsome, in the clear blue air,
The laverock sung his strains o' glee,
   And nature's heart was joyful there.

The lambs were bleating yont the knowes,
Where plaided herds roam'd pensively,
And wending south o'er heights and howes,
I pass'd the waters of the Dye.

Then glad I hail'd grey Dirrington –
The shelter of my sires of yore –
And trod the heath, oft trode upon
By men who Freedom's standard bore.

I left behind brown Lammermoor,
And, passing east from Cattleshiel,
I saw the Merse wide spread before,
And felt my heart with rapture reel.

Behind me lay the round bare hills,
The Laws which ne'er had felt the ploughs,
The pastoral slopes and wimpling rills,
The rushy bogs and ferny knowes.

The shepherd-sheiling, wild and lone,
The camps and cairns of ancient days,
I left them all, and hasten'd on,
To reach the Merse and Crunkly braes.

Dear native Merse! a glorious plain,
Streak'd wi' the sunbeams, mild and sweet;
I gaze far o'er thy fair domain,
Where true hearts in their gladness beat;

I come to tread thy fields again
Where long my fathers till'd thy soil,
And with thee and thy sons remain,
Till there I end life's ceaseless toil.

To Cheviot's border hills I turn,
O'er Teviotdale my view is cast;
On Flodden field I sigh and mourn,
And muse o'er days that long are past.

Far to the margin of the main
   See Halidon's grey skirts extend!
And wi' wild thoughts o' grief and pain,
   O'er Scotia's slaughtered sons I bend.

All that I love on earth is there,
   Land of my fathers! Happy land;
Be virtuous all thy daughters fair,
   And all thy sons in honour stand!

May tyrants and their minions flee
   Far from the Merse's bounds away!
May truth and genius dwell in thee!
   Thy toiling sons be glad for aye!

The land of Boston and M'Crie,
   Where Erskine preached and Baillie sung,
Where by the Leader's haughs and lea,
   The Rhymer's wizard harp was strung!

There, o'er thy waters, woods and rills,
   My heart will pour its warmest lay;
While morn and eve athwart thy hills,
   Shall all their varied charms display.

No land e'er blessed by sun or shower,
   Beneath the wide sky's azure dome,
Will e'er to me look half so fair
   As that which holds my my native home!

Though bleak and bare thy hills may be,
   Though winter tempests scathe thy plain,
O Merse! I could not part with thee,
   For all the gold beyond the main!

The shadows of the passing clouds,
   On Bunkle-edge sweep slowly by,
And o'er those scenes my memory broods,
   That struck my young enthusiast eye.

My heart still clings to native scenes,
   And cling it shall for ever more;
In thoughts by day, by night in dreams,
   I all their beauties wander o'er.

By woods and dells that skirt the Eye,
   'Midst heather bells, on moorlands bare,
In fancy, wandering lone, I hie,
   And sing their scenes and prospects fair.

Or down the hoary, rugged dean,
   'Mong sheltered rocks, with lichens grey,
I pluck the wild flowers, rarely seen,
   Or by Fast Castle's ruins stray.

Or o'er the wild St. Abbs I roam,
   Or down the Ale I wander slow,
And mark sweet Nature's every form,
   And drink her spirit as I go.

By haunted streams let me repose,
   In Pease's deep sequestered glen;
By fountains pure, in moss-grown howes,
   By limpid burn, or rushy fen.

O hide me in in the wildwood glade,
   Or lift me to yon moorlands brown,
Where, watching slow the sunlight fade,
   I'll see the autumn day go down.

In fond delight I gaze each morn
   O'er scenes that pleased my infant heart
And by the ripening, rustling corn
   I, lingering, muse and roam apart.

No other land I wish for mine
   Than my own fatherland – the best;
I there content will spend life's line,
   And in its soil my bones shall rest.

When silent o'er my wasting frame
   The green Merse sod will dewy lie,
Few then will e'er repeat my name,
   Yet o'er me still the winds will sigh,
And evenings mild, in distant years,
Will steep my grave with Nature's tears,
   And soothe my "pale shade" lingering nigh!

Undated – c.1830?

◇◇◇◇◇◇◇

Nature's Lament for Man's Encroachments

Our bonny burn-sides they hae drained and dug,
   The crooks o' the burn they hae altered too;
The green ferny knowes, where the hare lay snug,
   They hae cleared o' ilk buss, and riven wi' the pleugh.
The bonny green braes by the foggy dell,
   Where grew the broom and the black slae-thorn,
They hae levelled down wi' a purpose fell,
   And Nature laments a' her beauties torn.

The moor and the moss they hae a' ta'en in,
   To add to the great man's wealth and store,
And the green bog-land, where sykes did rin,
   Will bear the hay for our kye no more;
They hae torn up the sod o' the lang-syne fauld,
   And scattered the dust o' the hill-side cairn,
Where lay the bones o' the warriors auld,
   And Nature laments a' her beauties torn.

They hae choked up the well that flowed sae free,
  And the bonny well-strand they hae drained away,
Where young maiden Helen sang in her glee,
  Or hied wi' her full stoups up the brae.
Where flourished the rash-bush down i' yon howe,
  The barley rigs now wave there unshorn;
And there 'mong the rashes we'll nae mair rowe,
  Where Nature laments a' her beauties torn.

They hae torn up the knowes o' the foggy-bee,
  They hae scathed the bowers where the linties sang;
They hae broken up the brake o' the moory lea,
  Where the red blooms o' nature had blossomed lang;
They've stubbed up the briers on the green brae side,
  And changed the wild course o' our native burn;
And it's a' to keep up the great folks' pride –
  And Nature laments a' her beauties torn.

Thae hae houkit down the brae where the auld mill gaed,
  And the mill and the kiln are baith gane for aye;
And the bonny lound haugh where the bairnies played,
  Makes the big farmer's croft some bigger this day;
On the blaeberry bank where we haunted langsyne,
  The gloomy fir-trees are black i' the morn;
They hae dung down the bught and the grey mossy stane –
  And Nature laments a' her beauties torn.

It's not now at a' as it was langsyne,
  When the poor toiling man was his country's care;
Now the rich folk revel, and the poor folk pine,
  And the times are aye changing frae bad tae waur;
But the world may gang as it likes for me,
  If the green burn sides they wad keep frae corn,
And let a' the reeds and the rushes be,
  That Nature lament not her beauties torn.

But they've pu'd down the roof o' our fathers' ha',
  And laid bare its hearth to the winter cauld;
They've pleughed up the kail-yard, where roses did blaw,

And there lanely stand now the ash-trees auld;
The cottars are gane frae the auld steading, too,
And the wild soughing blast blaws owre it forlorn –
It's no like the place where our infancy grew –
And Nature laments a' her beauties torn.

Undated – c.1840?

◇◇◇◇◇◇◇◇

The Gude Auld Folk o' Little Billy

I've been where mony a burnie rows,
I've been beyond the Cowdenknowes,
I've been owre mony heights and howes,
And held the plough wi' mony a filly;
But whether I've gane by ha' or shiel –
Wherever I've gane to seek my meal,
I ne'er met folk I liked sae weel
As the gude auld folk o' Little Billy.

Sic mensfu' folk, in house or ha',
Sae true and leal, I never saw,
There ne'er was malice, guile, nor ga'
In the gude auld folk o' Little Billy.
They were nae folk o' muckle gear –
Proud haughty folk they couldna bear –
But plain and simple a' the year,
Were the gude auld folk o' Little Billy

Their bread and cheese were aye the best,
Their meat and meal aye stood the test,
For that – for a', they'll aye be blessed
The gude auld folk o' Little Billy.
The packman lad, and beggar man,
Lang Meg, Saut Samuel, and Geordie Tam,
And a' the wandering, houseless clan,
Gat aye some howf at Little Billy.

Pipers, fiddlers, and mugger chiels,
Came often there wi' cuds and creels,
And sometimes coupit up their heels
  About the auld wa's o' Little Billy.
Nae poor man there was e'er oppressed,
The poor had there aye peace and rest,
Friends to the poor they were the best –
  The gude auld folk o' Little Billy.

When they got a' their corn cut down,
They held their kirn – a merry stoun!
And blithely ranted through the town,
  Around the auld trees o' Litle Billy.
Auld barn- man Davie sang wi' glee,
And canty by the hallan was he,
And glanced on Lizzie wi' his ee
  'Mang a' the auld folk o' Little Billy.

Kind, hamely, social, frank, discreet,
Sic douce, leal folk I ne'er did meet,
And far owre swift my days did fleet
  Wi' the gude auld folk o' Little Billy.
The gudewife aye was neat and clean,
A working body, gleg and keen,
And blithe was she on croft and green,
  The leal gudewife o' Little Billy!

She carded woo', and darned, and span,
At swinglin' lint she tried her han',
And blithe at night was ilka one
  In the auld snug ha' o' Little Billy.
The gudewife span, the lasses sang,
Wi' bummin' wheels they aye were thrang,
And wha could e'er be sad or wrang,
  'Side the auld gudewife o' Little Billy?

Her webs she bleached by yon burnside –
Her webs and chuckies a' her pride ;
Her cheese could brag the country wide,
   And were aye a mense to Little Billy.
When yellow hues cam owre the corn,
To milk the yowes at early morn,
Her merry maids laughed care to scorn,
   And sang i' the bught at Little Billy.

And wha could match the gudeman true?
Sae mony things the man could do,
That in the Merse were very few,
   To match the gudeman o' Little Billy.
At ilka turn his hand was first,
Aye ready was he for ony birst,
A better worker ne'er was nursed
   Than the douce gudeman o' Little Billy.

In summer morn, in frost, and snaw,
He aye was up at the cock's craw,
And to his flock away did ca' –
   The gude auld man o' Little Billy.
But canny decent, honest folk
Are often crushed wi' this world's troke,
And leal, kind hearts are often broke
   Wi' a' this world's wrangs and folly.

But time is changing a' things here,
And changes mony we hae to fear,
And our gude friends had a' to steer
   Frae the auld snug ha' o' Little Billy.
And dowie now is yon burn brae,
Where bairns langsyne did sport and play,
And the clear well is drained away,
   Where drank the auld folk o' Little Billy.

Nae cot or ha' can now be seen
Where we sae happy oft hae been;
And a' the bairns hae left the green
Wi' the gude auld folk o' Little Billy.
Now soughing through the leafless trees
Loud sobs the chill November breeze;
Sic dreary scenes my fancy please,
Since they're a' away frae Little Billy.

Owre Bunckle Hill the storm drives fierce,
And sweeps along the withered Merse,
And through the boughs is wailing hearse,
O' the auld grey trees o' Little Billy:
A mournfu' dirge it seems to be
For those wha've gane frae croft and lea,
For them it mourns, who bore the gree
In the auld blithe hame o' Little Billy.

Undated – c.1840?

◇◇◇◇◇◇◇

The Maid of Danskein

Fair Helen sought Kilpalet[1] burn,
To wander sad and lonely there;
For oh, her heart was sair forlorn,
And nought could ease her bosom's care;
For he wha'd sworn to be her ain,
Had cruel, false and faithless been,
And grief untold, and ceaseless pain
Had wither'd a' her summer green.

Now sadly by Kilpalet burn
She roam'd amidst the gloamin' dew;
And sobs and tears did waste her form –
For Helen's heart was fond and true;
The gloamin' mist around her fell,
Where heathy wastes were wildly spread;

And lonely by the mossy well
She laid her grief-distracted head.

Low at her feet, Kilpalet burn
In soft sad murmurs lapsed away;
And on her bosom folds forlorn
The chill night dews did rest till day;
When dawning o'er the moorlands broke
She reach'd her home by Danskein Ha';
But joy no more her spirit woke –
For hopeless grief had claimed her a'.

Where shepherds, by Kilpalet burn,
Roam wi' their flocks the moorlands wide,
I'll sadly muse where wont to mourn
The shepherd's fair unwedded bride;
Beside the stream in woeful mood,
In Autumn's fitful changing day,
I'll sit and sigh for her – so good,
And pure as gowan on the brae.

'Twas there beside Kilpalet burn,
Her yellow locks wav'd on the gale;
But to that scene she'll ne'er return,
Nor woe again her heart assail;
Flow on lone stream, for ever flow –
She'll hear thy murmurs not again.
She sleeps the green grass sod below,
And's safe from sorrow, woe, and pain.

10 February, 1855. H.

[1] *A small mountain stream between Danskein and Longformacus, in Lammermoor.*

Jenny Snaw

Frae northern mountains far and vast,
Auld Jenny Snaw her mantle cast
In wreathing faulds upon the blast
And south away
By Labrador and Iceland past
Her stern array.

Scouring cross the stormy seas,
And o'er the misty Hebrides,
Frae Caledonia's mountain leas
Her brattling sledge
Came sounding on the icy breeze
To Buncle Edge.

Her slow and solemn pace was seen
Across the Lammermoors yestreen;
Wi' sleety hair and glancing een
I'd mark her thraw
Attour the Merse's level scene,
The drifted snaw.

In streaming mantle, lang and pale,
Glittering wi' gems, and dress'd wi' hail,
Owre frozen streams – through tempest's wail
I heard her come,
And skyte the beads frae aff her mail
Down *Davie's* lum!

Our little Nannie frae the loan
Came rinning in wi' hempy John,
The pirly hail her locks upon,
Crying "Mammy, see,
What Jenny Snaw, that elrich crone,
Has done to me!"

Wi' braid white flaughts upon the ground
She's scattered a' the fields around,
And drifted heaps in many a mound
Owre hill and glen,
And mony a cauldrife, pinching stound
She lets us ken.

Clear icicles hang frae her snout.
Her face is sad, and white's a clout,
Her numb blue hands hing shivering out;
Yet in her e'e
Mirth twinkles – and a blythsesome shout
She aft doth gie!

Though glistering cauld's her gaucy robe,
And fitful blasts around her sob,
And tears, in mony a frozen blob,
Her cheeks emboss;
Yet warmer heart's not on the globe –
Though sometimes cross.

On frozen dub, young Bob wi' glee
Is skiddin' by yon leafless tree,
Where hoary cranreuch owre the lea,
On rush and spray,
Makes *Jonny's* vesture sweet to me
This wint'ry day.

But when the night, descending fast,
Shuts up her gates far i' the west,
The wearied skaters homeward haste
To th' ingle side,
Where leal light hearts in blissful rest
And peace doth bide.

Warm, by our cozie ingle low,
I sat wi' calm contented brow,
Yet eye'd wi' joy the rosy glow
On faces bright,
And blessed the Power that fends us now
Ilk dreary night.

O bairns, remember now your state,
And gratefu' bless your happy fate,
And think how mony air and late
Maun toil and mourn,
And cauld and comfortless await
The Spring's return.

But Jenny, now you've lang been here,
Wi' a' your frozen, pouthery gear,
And fegs, we doubt you're unco sweer
Away to skyte –
The vera craws begin to fear
Ye hae gaen gyte!

O spare, ye limmer, spare the taes
O' the wee bairnies in duddy claes –
O mind yon matron down the braes,
Cow'rin' and thin,
Where dim her little spunk decays
The neuk within.

And mind yon lanely dowie dame,
Within her cauld and reeky hame,
Scorn'd by the world – in wae and shame
Her days are spent;
And every year wi' her's the same,
A time o' Lent!

Yon orphan band, wi' sorrow worn,
Fills me wi' wae ilk e'en and morn –
Now when frae them their stay is torn,
O pass their door!
And breathe not on their hearts forlorn
Thy tempest sore!

And Jenny, pass yon cottage by
Where Want and Sickness dim the eye,
Where pale Despair and Grief doth lie –
Blaw saftly there!
And come not wi' thy howlings nigh
The couch o' care.

Deep underneath thy fleecy hap,
Ye've smoor'd the sheep by yonder slap,
And thrown a fold owre Cheviot's tap
Besouth the Tweed;
And in the lone kirkyard ye lap
The silent dead!

What can thy bitter breath withstand? –
Thy withering, searing, saddening hand,
Spreads want and wae across the land –
O stay thy might,
And let the western breezes bland
Repair thy blight.

Dear Jenny Snaw! blaw not sae snell,
Thy freezing gars our fingers gell –
This year, you've wrought your cantrips well,
Now, go, I pray,
And let us hear the lav'rocks swell
Their chorus gay!

Ye drooping sons o' Toil and Want,
Wi' aumries toom, and pantries scant –
Bear up! – nor heed auld Jenny's vaunt –
March winds are near,
And soon will blaw her farewell rant,
Wi' blythesome cheer!

Back owre the hills wi' blirty swirl,
Her "adamantine car" will hurl,
And round our hame her growlin' gurl
Will sough nae mair;
And springing plants, and sang o' merle,
Will soothe our care.

Chirnside, February 24, 1855. H.

◇◇◇◇◇◇◇◇

The Text in the Snow

Verses on seeing the words "Cheer up" written upon the snow, by the roadside, near Whiterig, February 28, 1855.

O yes, cheer up! the star of hope
Is rising bright for thee,
And in a fairer, wider scope
Thy onward path will be.
Never despond – though toil and care
Press heavy on thy soul.
This life's a paltry poor affair,
And soon away must roll.

O yes, cheer up! though sad distress
And poverty be thine;
'Twill only make thy comforts less
To fret and to repine.
Never despond – though others go
Before thee in the race.
Though canst not fail if thou art low,
And keep an even pace.

O yes, cheer up! though proud ones jeer
And scorn thy humble state,
Be thou a Man – and never fear
The slanders of the great.
Never despond – though thousands rave,
And flout and tear thy name.
Keep thou the right, in virtue brave.
And where's the cause of shame?

O yes, cheer up! though reft and torn
Of all thy blessings here;
For darkest night there's brightest morn
A trusting heart to cheer.
Never despond – though faithless oft
Brothers and friends may be;
Trust not in man – but look aloft
Where blooms Life's fadeless tree!

O yes, cheer up! though baffled here
In all thy hopes and aims.
Thou'st done thy best – then all is clear,
And glorious are thy claims.
Never despond – though in life's war
Thou'st fallen by the way, –
The night will pass, and morn's bright star
Will herald happier day.

O yes, cheer up! let others shine
    In wealth and fashion fair.
Be good and noble thou, not fine,
    And on with true heart bear.
Never despond – life's wintery storms
    The free soul cannot blind,
And cruel oppression's blood-red forms
    Thou far shalt leave behind.

O yes, cheer up! though broken be
    Thy trust on all below;
Though homeless toss'd on land or sea,
    And steep'd in want and woe.
Yet ne'er despond! the stable Rock
    Will hold thine anchor fast,
And firm in tide and tempest's shock
    Thou'lt ride out every blast.

Chirnside, February 28, 1855. H.

◇◇◇◇◇◇◇◇

The Railway Engine

There goes the giant, terrific in might,
    The offspring of science, the boast of our day;
Fierce as the warrior, fleet as the gale,
    And woe to the wight that stands in his way.

For his brow is but sullen, his kindness sma',
    Nor piteous, nor sadly remorseful is he;
His iron-built frame is of sympathy void,
    And merciless too as the wild roarin' sea.

Yet a slave to mankind who seeks no repose,
    Nor season of rest with his labour and toil,
But gaily flies on with his motley crowd,
    And the ore and the wealth and the fruit o' the soil.

He snorts in the valley, he sweeps through the glen,
    Like a fiery courser the goal for to win;
He grapples with Time and conquers e'en space –
    What power upon earth can struggle with him.

Sires of antiquity! Could ye but come,
    And look once again on the valleys of earth,
How startled ye'd be at the work of our age,
    So unlike to whatever your genius gave birth.

Like the rush of the billow his voice it is heard,
    O'er the far distant hills at close o' the day.
When the echoes that ring in the warloch dells,
    On the wings of the zephyr are wafted away.

Go ransack the past with its art and its fame,
    Rake up its wonders, search where ye will,
What shall ye find that can once be compar'd
    With this grand achievement of science and skill!

For yonder he goes, terrific in might,
    The offspring of science, the boast of our day,
Fierce as the warrior, fleet as the gale,
    And woe to the wight that stands in his way.

Chirnside, March 31, 1855. G.

◇◇◇◇◇◇◇◇

Dunse Dings A'

Auld sober toun, hail! Blithely hail!
Lang may ye stand in that snug vale;
And though the bitter norlin' gale
        May loudly blaw,
Fu' cosie there ye sup your kail –
        Dunse dings a'.

Upon thy hills, wi' heather clad,
In days o' yore brave Leslie stood,
Wi' stern resolve for Scotland's guid
The sword to draw,
Till freedom raised its drooping head –
Dunse dings a'.

And still within that shelter'd glen
Are found the best o' honest men.
If there's a rogue ye've other ten
Without a flaw,
And sonsie queans baith but an' ben.
Dunse dings a'.

But waes my heart, that wee bit drappie,
Auld Scotland's ancient acquavitae,
That made our grand-dads aye sae happy,
Be't strong or sma',
Is there condemn'd 'thout hope or pity,
Dunse dings a'.

And dark and darker lours the storm
On puir abused John Barleycorn;
For now they've leagued, combined, and sworn
His neck to thraw,
And leave him helpless and forlorn.
Dunse dings a'.

Grey-bearded Custom, down he goes;
His drucken reign is near its close.
Auld Bacchus e'en his crown maun lose,
He's doom'd to fa'.
For owre his head wi' deadly blows
Dunse dings a'.

Even Moderation, lad o' grace,
Wi' straikit hair and sober face,
Daur scarcely rise to plead his case,
But snooves awa'.
To seek some mair congenial place.
Dunse dings a'.

Ye drouthy louns that's drunkards been,
Degraded, filthy, low and mean,
Come wash in Jordan and be clean,
And busk ye braw;
Their final cure's the mountain stream.
Dunse dings a'.

Down, down your stoups and bumpers fling,
And leave that sinfu' jovial ring,
Walk circumspect, nor funk nor fling,
In house or ha';
Then jolly fun its dirge may sing,
Dunse dings a'.

O publicans, ye weel may mourn,
Your day is past, your hairst is shorn,
Bauld spokesmen here, wi' genius born,
Whom fame ne'er saw,
Blaws declamations' loudest horn.
Dunse dings a'.

But ye wha' want a lawyer chiel
To plead your cause and plead it weel,
Your grievance lang ye needna feel
Nae time ava',
Ye've birkies here wad gliff the deil.
Dunse dings a'.

Chirnside, April 1855. G.

Maggie Methven – A Song

Tune – "Come row me owre to Charlie"

I'll owre the Myre to yonder mill,
I'll owre the Myre to Maggie;
I'll up, and owre the Staineshiel hill,
And through the Myre to Maggie.

Their day's work done, the eventide,
Is sweet unto the weary;
But longing hearts are sleepless eyed –
I long to meet my dearie!
I'll owre the Myre, &c.

The shade o' gloamin's on the lea,
My bonnet's on the knaggie,
And while the bat around doth flee
I'll steal away to Maggie.
I'll owre the Myre, &c.

The moon is up – the wind is loun',
The mist fills a' yon vale now,
And owre the Nunbutts I am boun'
To tell my true love tale now.
I'll owre the Myre, &c.

The Myre they say's a haunted place,
Wi' reeds and willows wavin';
But ghaists will never turn my face
When gaun to Maggie Methven!
I'll owre the Myre, &c.

Our trysting- place the well shall be
That trickles through the cresses;
And there my love will prove to me
A fount of raptur'd blisses.
I'll owre the Myre, &c.

Sweet are her looks, wi' gowden hair
    Owre neck and bosom hingin';
Her lips – O what a treasure's there,
    And bless'd be she that bore her!
                I'll owre the Myre, &c.

Her heart is leal – her love sincere,
    And fondly I adore her;
She's a' the wealth I care for here,
    And bless'd be she that bore her!
                I'll owre the Myre, &c

Chirnside, April 23, 1855. H.

◇◇◇◇◇◇◇

Helen

How sweet among the morning dew,
The gowan's rosy tip to view!
And sweet in May's bright balmy morn,
To see the gay green springing corn!
But many a year has come and gane
Since Helen view'd the smiling plain,
And since frae aff its wiry stem
She pluck'd the gowan's "bonny gem."

Far in the azure vault aboon,
The laverock chirles a cheery tune;
And down beside yon smiling wood,
The lintwhite charms the solitude:-
But flower, or birds, or blooming trees,
Nae mair my Helen's heart can please,
For low she lies in endless rest,
The green grass waving o'er her breast.

The mother, and the sire are there –
That mother, who sorrowed o'er thee sair;
That hoary sire how meekly bore
Life's toils and cares that broke him sore;
And there ye lie a' side by side,
Till Time shall stay his troublous tide,
And soon, O Helen, soon wi' thee
We'll rest, from a' life's sorrows free.

Chirnside, June 9, 1855. H.

◇◇◇◇◇◇◇

An Ode to the Corn-Crake

Welcome, bird of early summer,
Lively, gladsome, happy comer!
How leaps my heart anew to hear
Down in the crofts thy harping clear.

When the gloaming's balmy hand,
Scatters the pearls across the land,
And in the west the cloudlets dim,
Are glowing with a crimson rim,
Then gladly on mine ear doth fall
Thy sweetly rural, happy call.

Pleasing ay thy strain has been,
Happy crake! on ridges green:
To the tender, feeling heart
Peaceful thoughts thy strains impart;
To the soul that's true and leal
Nature's heart thou dost unseal;
Keenly harping night and day,
Like a Poet on his lay,
Never tiring of thy theme,
Sweeter ne'er could mortal deem!

From the morn until the noon,
Thou art working at thy tune;
From the noon until the eve,
Thou thy harping wilt not leave!
All the night, amidst the corn,
Harping to the vales forlorn,
Cheering the wayfarer lone,
To his fire-side hastening on;
And the lover, hieing fain
O'er the dew-besprinkled plain,
To his fair one in the west,
Where his heart shall find its rest,
Clinging close to Ellen's breast!

When I wander forth at night,
Hid from every mortal's sight,
Tracing the dim paths along,
Sweeter then I love thy song;
Sweeter then I love to hear,
In the furrows echoing near,
Voices which my soul doth fill.

When the wind sleeps on the hill,
And the summer time of bloom
Wafts abroad a sweet perfume,
Hidden 'mong the grass or wheat,
Thy joys are perfect and complete;
And though thou to mortal e'en
Art ever shy of being seen –
What car'st thou for mortal's love
Or that they should'st thee approve?

What reck'st thou of busy men,
Toiling still in Mammon's den,
Striving, straining, high and low,
To keep up a plausive show,
Working hard at vanities,
And their bargains, gains and lies! –
Better far in glory singing,

O'er the rigs thy harp is ringing;
Better far, and purer, thou
Harpest on the clover knowe;
And every strain of thine is sweeter
Than the poet's happiest metre.
Sure thou hast a poet's spirit,
And evermore shalt joy inherit!

O happy crake! could I with thee
Ever a companion be,
Nestling down among the clover,
With the sweet lark singing over,
Pouring forth a raptured strain
O'er the verdant, dewy plain,
Drinking ay from Nature's breast
Balmy sweets that bring us rest,
Listening to the soothing measures,
And the voice of rural pleasure,
And the ceaseless, sighing hum,
That through grass and corn doth come! –
There we'd harp and sing together,
All the blessed summer weather,
Till the harvest-time was near,
Then we'd seek another sphere,
In some region, calm and old,
Far from withering care and cold,
O'er the dark-tempestuous main,
In an ever-green domain!

Happy bird! No fretting care
Ever dims thy prospects fair;
Thine is all a life of bloom,
Sorrow never stains thy plume;
No day hast thou that's sad or dull,
Of gladness ay thy heart is full;
'Midst the fresh green springing corn
Thou art happy night and morn.
Singing in thy *present* joy,
The *future* gives thee no annoy.

Sunny days, in furrows green,
Thou can'st spend in joy serene;
Night, when nature's steeped in dew,
Still thy raptures doth renew;
And no night or day to thee
Lessens aught of joy or glee;
O' were our souls but tun'd like thine,
Never would we grieve or pine,
And no weariness or woe
Would our hearts e'er overflow!

Blessed be the gracious Arm
Sent thee here our fields to charm!
He gives us corn, grass, and flowers,
And heat, and fertilising showers;
And birds to sing his praises sweet,
In the bowers with joy complete.

All the world's a glorious book,
On which we with delight may look;
And every flower, and bird, and fly
Point us to the Power on high;
Primrose, daisy, crake and lark
Show us here His handiwork,
Speaking in a language clear
Of His will to bless our sphere,
And make the sons of men rejoice
In His kind paternal voice;
If He for birds takes such a care
Shall not *man* his goodness share?
Then in His works – and endless store, –
We'll rejoice for evermore!

Chirnside, June 7, 1855. H.

On the Death of Dr. Geo. Johnston of Berwick-Upon-Tweed

"Allow me to throw a Flower upon his grave"

SAD, sorrowing friends in anguish mourn,
And droop desponding o'er his urn.
Science deplores and sighs forlorn
O'er his loved bier,
And weeping cries, "He'll ne'er return,
Our hearts to cheer."

In Nature's service, warm, sincere,
He toiled with zeal from year to year;
And while he spoke with wisdom clear,
Her pages shone;
Now darker shades oppress our sphere,
Since he is gone.

Refreshed with Flora's varied sweets,
He frequent stole to her retreats,
Where life's sharp woes and gilded cheats
Were left behind;
And far from Trade's long crowded streets,
Great wealth he'd find.

Dear to his heart earth's wilding flowers;
Her wastes, her streams, her sylvan bowers,
The glad sunshine, and fresh'ning showers,
He loved them all:
And in earth's many voiced powers
He found no gall.

All Nature's aspects, forms and hues, –
Her cheering smile when Spring renews
Earth's verdant breast with pearly dews,
He hail'd serene:

And Winter even did joy infuse
Through's spirit keen.
The countless treasures of the deep,
That swim unseen, or silent creep,
He searched out – and rocky steep,
Or level shore,
Were wealthy fields, where oft he'd reap
A glorious store.

The gorgeous bird, the gilded fly,
Were charming to his heart and eye.
Green river side, and mountain high,
He roam'd with joy;
And plants and shells did thoughtfully
His powers employ.

He loved to plough the furrows o'er
Where scattered lies our ancient lore,
And deep in classic mines explore
For gems of thought,
Which bygone times laid up in store –
Though seldom sought.

But while devoted night and day
To Science, or the Muses' lay,
From Duty's path he would not stray,
But stern did cope
'Gainst dire disease and pain's fell sway
With life-strang hope.

With cheerful mood life's path he trode,
And, strong in soul, bore sorrow's load,
In virtue firm, with faith in God
He ran his race;
And now he's reach'd Life's fair abode,
And Love's embrace!

Addiction's sons will miss him sore,
The poor their lost friend will deplore,
And modest merit droop before
The stroke of fate –
And lamp gone out, to shine no more
On earth's low state!

Yet he his day hath spent right well,
And left precious works to tell
Of beauties that in Nature dwell; –
Those books will bide,
And bear his name with gentle spell,
Down Time's far tide.

We mourn the sage, to rest gone down,
Through blessings shall his memory crown –
All Nature seems to mourn her own
In silent pain.
O Friend beloved! Since thou art gone,
How few remain!

May wild flowers deck thy verdant grave,
Red thyme, and bluebells o'er thee wave,
And heaven's soft dews for ever lave
Thy place of rest!
For thee, lover of Nature! Now we crave
Peace in her breast!

Chirnside, 1 August, 1855. H.

Dr George Johnston was a founder member, and first President, of the Berwickshire Naturalists' Club. Ed.

A Response to the Address of St. Abb's Head to his Good Friends, the Public

"When rocks and stones begin to cry,
'Tis time our hearts were rous'd thereby."

O famed St. Abbs, I greet thee well,
Rising above the ocean's swell
Wi' rugged front, thou bear'st the bell,
Owre Headlands a';
And, troth, you've nicely learn'd to spell,
Since I you saw.

Thy aff-hand crack I like to hear;
It shows a spirit cold and clear,
And now, I think, we needna fear
By thee to stand,
Let lords and lairds their birses rear –
Hae, there's my hand!

Shall we not hae a right to roam
Where thy auld kirk looked on the foam,
In ancient days – aince the lone home,
O sainted Ebba;
And never more thy features goam
Auld farrant gabbie?

When mist and vapour shade thy brow,
And in the blast the wild curlew
Screams high aboon thy dusky hue,
O how sublime
The troubled ocean's breast to view
Frae thy high clime!

And when the saft warm breezes blaw
Owre thy bare scalp – and sweet showers fa';
And wake the flowers sae peerless braw
On thy green slopes,
Shall we be barr'd to view them a'
Wi' fresh young hopes?

Let a' sic thoughts far banish'd be –
Nae "grasping laird" shall dim your ee;
Nor dowie down thy grassy lee
Let saut tears rin;
For we'll be wi' you in our gree,
Baith kith and kin!

We'll haud our "pic-nics" on your braes,
Let great men gloom, and prove thy faes;
We'll keep unscath'd our "right o ways"
For times to come;
We're Scotchmen yet! – and high's our praise
In many a home.

Then bare thy cantle to the sky,
My bauld St. Abbs! and waving high
Our banners yet shall cheer thine eye,
When on yon steep
Where we, as in the day gone by,
A feast will keep!

The raging sea, for ages lang,
Has lash'd thy feet wi' surges strang,
While thou, and mariners, bore the bang,
O wintry weather
And fishers saw the tempests strang
Around thee gather.

Our bauld forefathers, lang syne dead,
Hae often watch'd about thy Head,
To see white vessels onward speed
About the main; –
O' canker'd lairds they had nae dread,
For fear was nane.

The lairds, lang syne, were better men,
Than bar our folks frae shore or glen;
And sure, they were nae poorer then,
That our forebears
View'd nature's scenes by lock or fen –
O' law nae fears.

And shall their bairns hae nae access
Around thy hoary pow to press?
And shall their rights grow less and less
Some laird to please?
Confound the craven heart wad mess,
Wi' thoughts like these!

No hearty Cock! We'll ne'er gie in,
As lang's we hae a bit o' skin!
And bravely we our "way" will win;
And keep it too –
Let lairds gang gyte, and rampant rin
We'll stand by you!

Oh dear St. Abbs! I'll love thee aye,
Though thy auld Head is hoary gray;
My soul's been cheer'd to pass the day
By thy wild steep,
And view the tempest track its way
Across the deep.

By thee, auld Cock! We'll stand or fa!
Brave border lads and lasses braw.
And wives and bairns will crousely craw
About thee yet;
For right, and liberty, and law
We a' are set.

Then take nae fear, auld neighbour stern,
Our hearts for thee will ever yearn
And since wi' a' thy woes did learn
We've been right sad
That men should 'gainst our friendship girn
And ca' us mad!

Men o' the Merse! Sons o' the sea!
Wi' ane accord stand to your plea,
Make to *St. Abbs* a pathway free,
Bear nae defeat!
And for your bairns win liberty,
For Ebba's seat.

Chirnside, March 15, 1856. H.

◇◇◇◇◇◇◇◇

Blythe Maggie is the Lass for Me

Young Willie was a gardener bred,
Ken'd ilka leaf and flower that sprang,
And oft he vowed he ne'er wad wed,
But sober thoughts are sometimes wrang;
For now he says, "Gae mak' a sang,
And let the burden o' it be –
Whate'er my lot, where'er I gang,
Blythe Maggie is the lass for me."

"But Willie there's a book of fate,
What's written there nae tongue can tell;
Perchance some other gentle mate
Is destined here wi' you to dwell;"
"Grim fate may keep her to himsel'
Nor tease me wi' his fell decree:
Till time sound my departing knell,
Blythe Maggie is the lass for me."

"But yon braw lad that tends the flock,
And Jonnie Liddel on the main,
At Maggie's window oft did knock,
And will they never come again?"
"Nae, nae – she'll soon be a' my ain,
Her heart an' han' nae longer free,
And suitors a' may sue in vain,
Since Maggie is the lass for me."

"Wow! courtship, lad, is charming still,
'Tis poetry ilk word that flows,
But wedlock's said to break the spell,
And then comes sober sullen prose."
"O may the powers his weel oppose,
Wha tells this wicked wilfu' lee,
For ne'er a spark my flame shall lose,
When blythesome Maggie's wed to me."

Chrinside, September 1, 1856. G.

The Howe o' Winter

In the howe o' winter cauld
When the winds blaw loud and snell;
When the snaw lies i' the fauld,
And sear leaves i' the dell;
When owre the chimla-taps
The soughin' blast yells keen,
And misty cloud enwraps
The auld grey hills, at e'en.

Then come ye bairnies mine,
And round the ingle draw;
And there ye'll cozy a' recline,
Though Boreas fiercely blaw.

Let frost the burns congeal,
And drift blaw owre the plain;
Nae frost ye here will feel,
Nae bitter cauld or rain;
There's nae shelter i' the shaw;
Nae bield upon the moor;
On leafless trees, the craw
Sits in the winter stoor.
Then come, &c.

And courin' by the dikes,
The flocks and hirsels bide
A' night without the tykes,
While owre the country wide
The cauld and darkness brood;
And deep in dreary dells
The streamlet brattles loud,
And on the night-breeze swells.
Then come, &c.

Let wint'ry wreaths lie lang,
In howes o' *Lauderdale*;
Let drifts, wi' whiddering bang

Drive owre the *Merse's* vale;
Owre heath-clad *Lammermoor*,
Wild rave the stormy blast,
But warm's your theekit bower,
And lang sae may it last!
Then come, &c.

The tod upon the hill,
The rabbit in the dean,
Hae little there to fill
Their hungry maws at e'en;
Now mutely sits the lark
On frozen furrows, low,
While wavering in the dark,
Aboon her sweeps the snow.
Then come, &c.

In halls and chambers bright,
The great may dance at e'en;
And in the city's light,
The rich and gay convene;
But there's gladness sweeter far,
In some lone country glen,
If there's nae pride to mar,
The peace o' rural men.
Then come, &c.

Wi' health and country joy,
Ye bairnies be content,
And may nae black annoy
Be on your bosom spent!
In the howe o' winter cauld,
Your bields be cozy ay;
And wi' the frail and auld
Be blithe as birds in May!
Then come, &c.

Chrinside, 22 January, 1857. H.

Polwart on the Green

A New Song to an Auld Tune

As I was bound for Greenlaw town,
Wi' weary feet and sair,
I grieved to see the sun gang down,
Ere I was half-gate there;
But soon my sorrow changed to glee,
As soon as I had seen
The bonny face o' Marion Lee,
At "Polwart on the green."

I sat wi' her, I drank wi' her,
Till dawin o' the morn;
Set a' the gairy folk asteer
To gang and shear the corn;
We danced wi' merry hearts and free
As ever yet had been –
But the blythest lass was Marion Lee,
At "Polwart on the green."

The jolly herd o' Choicelea town
Wi' kent and colly came;
Frae Cattleshiel, owre heather brown,
A rosy moorland dame;
The miller lad frae Polwart mill,
Came brankin' owre the dean,
And muckle glee their hearts did fill
At "Polwart on the green."

Frae Sisterpath young Peggy Shiel,
Wi' her bonny yellow hair,
Gaed linkin' briskly through the reel –
The fairest o' the fair;
And ploughman Tam frae Ladyflat,
A souple lad and clean,
Gar'd lasses hearts gang pity-pat,
At "Polwart on the green."

Frae Polwart Bents came maidens twa,
    The brawest o' them a';
But Marion did sae gently gae,
    She sham'd the fine and braw;
And never back to Greenlaw town
    I'll gang wi' purpose keen,
For Marion Lee has held me boun'
    At "Polwart on the green."

Lang syne they danc'd about the thorn,
    Baith lads and lasses fair;
And merry in the moonlight born
    Was love and music there;
And never since in cot or ha'
    Was sic a pleasant scene,
As when I, Marion, dancing saw
    At "Polwart on the green."

The ladies and the lairds langsyne
    Danc'd round the Polwart thorn,
And they, nae doubt, were very fine,
    Ere Marion Lee was born;
But now, I'll brag the warld wide,
    The mighty and the mean,
For ane wha could surpass my bride,
    At "Polwart on the green."

The lads and lassies o' the Merse
    In love and fun are free,
And tho' lovely queens are naewise scarce,
    There's nane like Marion Lee;
And what is better far than a',
    Leal is her heart I ween,
And bless'd the day I Marion saw
    At "Polwart on the green."

Chirnside, 28 February, 1857. H.

A Call for Spring

Come, ye soft Hesperian breezes,
Blow your fresh'ning breath again;
Strong desire my heart now seizes
To salute you on the plain;
Heard you not the laverock pouring
His rejoicing, raptured lay,
While the sun's bright beams were showering
O'er green rigs and fallows grey?

I have seen the lapwing bounding
O'er the furrows newly-sown;
And the cushet's voice resounding,
Echoes through the woodland lone;
Yonder white sea-mews are winging
Inland far, their gladsome flight;
While the shilfas and linnets singing
Fill the hedges with delight.

Busy rooks are ceaseless cawing
Round their ancient brooding trees;
And the shepherds, since the dawning,
Have been out upon the leas;
New-come lambs are sporting rarely
By their fleecy dams at noon,
O'er the green mounds skipping fairly,
There they patter round and roun'.

I have seen the sweet primroses,
In the dells and dingles deep,
Peeping forth among the mosses
From their chilly winter sleep;
And the red-tipt, lowly gowan
Sunward turns its bosom fair,
Where yon glassy stream is rowin'
O'er the sand and pebbles rare.

Ploughmen up the sloping ridges,
    Urge their team in hopeful glee,
While along yon woodland edges,
    Tassel'd hazels skirt the lea;
Silvery "palms" on willows gleaming,
    Sweetly o'er the waters bend;
And all 'round is nature teeming
    With a freshness, without end.

Buds on briers, in deans are swelling,
    Hawthorn buds are bursting too;
Round the wren's green mossy dwelling,
    Springeth up the violets blue;
Yellow gems the meadows flushing
    Tell of God's paternal care;
Where the rills are onward gushing,
    Blooms the golden pilewort fair.

On the blossom'd willows humming,
    Hear the wild bees happy strain,
Telling of bright days acoming –
    Days of Flora's blooming train!
Bells and blossoms, many-tinted,
    Banks and braes shall richly strow, –
God hath all this wide earth planted
    Both for use and beauty too.

Children, steeped in want and sorrow,
    Pinch'd with winter's cheerless gloom,
Go ye forth, when comes the morrow,
    Watch the flowerets in their bloom:
If the God, who brings the seasons,
    Clothe the flowers in such array,
Shall not He, for better reasons,
    Care for you, O faithless, say?

O how sweet the western breezes
Fans the verdant-braided corn!
All the sun-lit landscape pleases
At the fresh-dew'd, early morn;
Sprinkled o'er the tender clover,
Dew-drops, pure as heaven, repose;
So your Father's hand shall cover
With his blessing, all your woes.

Chirnside, March 26, 1857. H.

◇◇◇◇◇◇◇◇

The Glen where Tibby Dwelt

Down in the glen where Tibby dwelt,
I oft hae woo'd my winsome dearie,
And a' the sweets o' love hae felt,
Where Tibby kept up sic a steerie.

My bonny Peggie owre yon hill,
There's nane but me is wooin' at her;
Courtin' her wi' vigour still,
And not a man but me will get her.

I've wander'd wi' her owre the knowes,
Where happy birds their music utters,
Where Tibby Fowler milk'd her ewes,
And gathered gear to plague her suitors.

As sitting by the Bastel-Tae,
And musing on beside the water,
We saw her wooers climb the brae,
A' raving madly to be at her.

Glee'd cripple Jock o' Eddrington,
Weel mounted on his naig did blatter;
But he fell off and tint his shoon,
And waes my heart! he never got her.

Black blinkin' Tam o' Clarabad,
    Wi's new plush breeks did proudly caper,
But something scaur'd his bausuit yaud,
    And he flew off like misty vapour.

Lang Roger Sim wi' muckle pride,
    Wi' barkint boots, came frae the Spittal;
But Tibby set his claim aside,
    And he cut his thrapple wi' his whittle.

Young tarry-breeks o' Foulden town,
    Aye thought himself a lad o' metal,
But Tibby's scowl maist knock'd him down,
    And he fell owre the parritch-kettle!

Poor dusty Bob o' Lamb's Mill, fell
    Out owre the lugs wi' Tibby's tocher,
But wi' the parritch-stick itsel'
    She daiver'd Bob for sic an offer.

At een gaed stiltin down the glen,
    The girnin' dominie o' the Clappers;
But Tibby wi' the leister en'
    Soon gar'd the dominie use his flappers.

Grey Watty Ramsay o' the brae,
    The bien auld laird o' Foulden Bastel,
For Tibby's love did sigh and pray,
    But she was deaf as Norham castle.

The scrievin' lads o' Paxton town,
    A' rowin' came across the water,
But ere the rising o' the moon,
    She sent them home wi' weary swatter.

Black "Tibby Fowler o' the Glen,"
    Had mony wooers for her siller,
But she wed wi' ane she didna ken,
    Wha soon wi' mony waes did fill her.

A haffet lock o' Peggy's hair,
For a' the wealth o' Tibby Fowler
I wadna gie, I here declare,
She let her gear for ever moul'er.

Chirnside, April, 1857. H.

◇◇◇◇◇◇◇

Extempore Lines on the Late Unfavourable Weather

Lang raws o' stooks are drenched seen,
A' weather-beat, and growing green,
The aits, and barley, wheat and beans
Are ga'en to wrack –
Neist year we'll a' be unco lean –
Hearts like to crack.

Wet to the skin amang the stooks,
We gang a' day wi' waesome looks,
Like drookit craws, or heartless rooks,
The sheaves to set up,
And lang for night and cozy nooks,
And hearths weel het up.

The crap is gane, beyond remead,
It's fit for neither seed nor bread,
And parritch thin, we'll hae indeed
For years ensuin',
Our inwards will get mony a screed,
And run to ruin.

On mauten'd bread and claggy brose
It's hard to live – and sic a dose,
Ilk night and morn, you may suppose
                Will scour us sma',
And grips, and aches, and granes, and woes,
                Confound us a'.

Our heart and soul wi' wonder's struck,
To see yirth's produce turned to muck,
And soon right low will sink our pluck,
                When craps thus fail,
And wretched is a Scotchman's luck,
                Without his kail.

Ah, waes my heart! for a' this trouble,
As fushionless as rotten stubble
The strae will be – our beasts will grubble
                Cauld winter through,
But poorly on sic fodder – a bubble,
                This crap's I trow!

Our sins, I fear, do scourge us sair –
Our pride, our lust, our cry for mair,
Our love o' wealth – our fashions fair,
                Our vile conceit –
Are stinking rank 'maist everywhere –
                Our pride is great.

And pride maun fa' – ordained by fate –
Repent, ye sinners, ere too late,
In humble trust God's mercy wait,
                Ca' canny ay,
And Providence will bless you yet,
                And be your stay.

And whether crops are good, or nane,
Brought soundly in, or soaked wi' rain,
If ye frae vice will not refrain,
But spend the whole
On selfish ends – your peace is gane,
And lost's your soul!

Boast not, ye men o' wealth and power;
Culture is good – but sun and shower
Is sent by God, and small and sour
Wad be th' increase,
If He withheld to bless ilk hour,
Your wealth wad cease.

Be wise – nor ride wi' ruinous haste
Oure those below in fortune placed,
Nor earth's rich fruits in riot waste,
Mild be your rule,
And ye'll be ne'er wi' curses chas'd
To Stygian pool!

Chirnside, September 12, 1857. H.

◇◇◇◇◇◇◇◇

The Year's Decline

(Written in an hour of dejection)

A sadness o'er my spirit steals,
To see the leaves decay;
And fancy, to the soul reveals
The cold, bleak winter day.

The hips along the wayside hedge,
Assume a bright red hue,
And on yon brae's wild craggy ledge,
Still wave the witch-bells blue.

Upon the steep, all shining bright,
    The rowans cluster red,
While jetty brambles, ripe, in sight
    Along the banks are spread.

Few flowers to cheer our hearts, remain
    On meadows, moor, or wold,
And fields are swept of all their grain,
    The furrows damp and cold.

A woeful moaning's in the breeze,
    A deep, and solemn wail,
While harping through the scathed trees,
    Grief's fingers there prevail.

Low, mournful sounds across the moors,
    At evening's hour pass on;
And o'er the hill the mist-wreath lours
    On lated wanderer lone.

The friends, we early lost, return
    In twilight visions dim;
The long departed ones we mourn
    When sung's the evening hymn.

And, starting to the eye, the tear
    In bitterness, rolls down;
And sad, regretful thoughts, we bear
    For earthly prospects flown.

Like withered leaves in autumn's day
    Our hopes and joys are shed,
Swept by the reckless blast away,
    And scattered 'mongst the dead.

And soon this mortal frame in night,
    And mouldering grave will lie,
And nature's glories, fair and bright,
    Be hidden from our eye.

From nature's joys, from kindred torn,
In darkness deep, and still,
We'll hail no more the summer morn,
Or walk by fount or rill.

Green o'er our head the sod will grow,
The winter rains descend,
And years and seasons, in their flow,
Will never have an end!

O' dismal view! – perpetual death,
Oblivion's pall untorn!
Away grim thoughts! come cheering faith,
And wake the eternal morn!

Live in the future's glorious day –
My soul, exult and sing!
Speed time upon thy destin'd way,
And bliss perpetual bring!

Blow on, ye winds! And scatter all
The year's bright gems away;
Let winter's gloom in misery fall,
O'er nature's aspect grey;

But resting firm, in faith and hope,
That all shall spring anew;
My heart will 'gainst misfortune scope
And wade all misery through!

Chirnside, September 17, 1857. H.

The Fall of the Leaf

On Ninewall groves declining day,
In golden gleams now dies away;
And fading woods a varied scene
Are gilded with a glow serene;
With solemn thoughts impressed, I view
The paths, which withered leaves bestrew,
The paths where our forefathers trode
Along life's weary, chequered road;
And think, that we like them will soon
To the cold grave be shaken down.

The yellow leaves which strew the dell,
When Autumn blows his wild farewell,
Are types of man's decaying race,
When drooping age, with palid face,
And hoary locks, and faltering pace,
And wrinkled cheek, and misty eye,
His mind depress, and make him sigh,
For brighter years and seasons past,
And hopes and joys that faded fast;
The green, the fresh, the flowery bloom
Of life is gone – and to the tomb
We're hastening on with rapid speed,
And soon must sink among the dead;
Our names forgot – our memory gone,
Or only spelt on mossy stone,
Where lie the mouldering heaps of dust,
In churchyard green, that keeps in trust,
Our ashes till the awful morn,
When all must rise to bless or scorn –
To weal or woe – to joy or pain,
That ever must unchanged remain.

Like autumn leaves we drop today,
And pass from all we love away;
In death's long sleep in silence rest,
The verdant turf above us press'd,

While heedless o'er our prostrate clay,
Life's busy sons press on the way,
While gilded phantoms all pursue,
And few or none have truth in view.
Poor, vain, deluded, bustling men,
How low the aims ye here may ken;
How groveling, vile, and senseless still,
We wander on with perverse will!
And rarely till the last we've seen,
How vain our wayward course has been,
Then down we drop like falling leaves,
And few for our decease e'er grieves.

Sweet beams of day's departing hours,
On Ninewell's yellow fading bowers,
O could my life's last days decline,
So calm, so sweet as rays of thine,
On nature, in this placid hour,
That owns a blessed, benignant power,
And sink with wan leaves in the ground,
And sleep, my long, long sleep profound,
Till the last morn awake the just,
To sing their glory, hope and trust!

Chirnside, October 31, 1857. H.

Cauld Winter Weather

When 'midst his snow drifts Boreas sits,
Or maniac like prevailing,
Across the moors he raves by fits,
In voice o' dreary wailing; –
Then sweet it is, when day is done,
To meet wi' friend and brother,
Around the fire, for lack o' sun,
In cauld winter weather.
The toiling wight works hard a' day,
And little gear he gathers;
And oftentimes his heart is wae
Amid his fears and swithers;
But glad at een, he hameward steers
Wi' heart maist light's a feather;
When spousal smiles his bosom cheers,
In cauld winter weather.

Barefooted wretch! see yonder child,
On frozen paths lone-straying,
While waving in the breezes wild,
Her loose lint-locks are playing:
When round the board, in reveling glee,
Ye rich ones nightly gather –
O mind sic poor ones – ere they die
In cauld winter weather!

In darksome cots sad widows sit,
Dejected and forsaken,
While round their sair hearts grief is knit,
And a' their hopes down-shaken: –
Ye generous souls! who hae the power,
Go to sic hame together,
And cheer pale Misery's squalid bower
In cauld winter weather!

While at the jovial bowl ye keep,
    Ye careless ones, till morrow,
Many are tossing on the deep,
    And exiles sigh in sorrow:
O think of those who wander long,
    And ne'er 'mong friends can gather,
To join your social crack or song
    In cauld winter weather!

While streams are bound by icy bands,
    And Nature shrinks despairing,
There's One on high the storm commands;
    Who aye for Man is caring.
Then let us ne'er despond while here,
    Though cares and woes come hither,
Our trust in God will banish fear
    In cauld winter weather!

Many the ills that round us twine,
    Our bosom joys depressing,
And many woes and wars combine
    To make our times distressing:
But times may change – though lowering now –
    And dark clouds round us gather,
As Spring will drive frae Cheviot's brow,
    The cauld winter weather!

Chirnside, 11 February, 1858. H.

Spring has Come

"In my breast
Spring awakens too: and my regret
Becomes an April violet,
And buds and blossoms like the rest." – *Tennyson*

On roll the years – we older grow,
But are we wiser yet?
The head of age is clothed in snow,
    The past we oft regret;
But 'midst a train of doubts and fears,
We hail with joy the coming years,
    And forth in hope we go.

On roll the years! the Spring again
    Revives the earth's perfume,
And on the hill, and on the plain
    Unnumbered daisies bloom;
Beneath the bush, in sheltered nook,
The violets peep with modest look,
    Amidst the vernal rain.

The yellow coltsfoot o'er the lea,
    In golden bloom comes forth,
While merry lapwings bounding flee
    Cold winters to the north –
The lambkins skip o'er ridges green,
And shepherds hail the smiling scene,
    Of moral peace and glee.

The sweet primrose, and pilewort gay
    Spring beauteous from the sod;
On grassy plots sits the young May,
    And gladness flings abroad;
While through the wood with sweet amaze
The cuckoo's note 'mid noontide haze,
    Recalls life's early day.

The Spring has come! with dewy feet
    She's passed the woodland glade,
And waked the fragile wind-flower sweet,
    And gem'd each grassy blade.
The wood-sorrel too appears again,
Pure, pale and white with purple vein,
    Drooping on mossy seat.

In gentle breezes, waving high,
    The birches tassels swing;
While trilling free, in cloudless sky,
    The larks their anthems sing;
And 'midst the boughs of budding trees
Is heard the boom of wilding bees –
    In dells the cushets cry.

The years roll on, with ceaseless wheel
    The seasons come and go;
God's truth and wisdom they reveal,
    His goodness ever show;
In all the ages past and gone,
The God of Nature from His throne,
    On Nature sets His seal.

And all the tract of future years
    His hand their course will guide;
The stamp Divine all nature bears
    On hill and valley wide;
And waving far the golden corn
Clothes the fair fields at dawn of morn,
    Whereon man's hopes abide.

O let all human hearts awake
    To Nature's wonderous voice,
Shake from their breasts the coiling snake
    Of sloth – and aye rejoice;

See God's great book wide open laid,
With bud and bloom, and light arrayed,
And laced with stream and lake.

The teeming earth by sun and shower
In glory shines serene,
And bright and glad comes forth the flower,
With wheat and barley green;
Let gladness fill the breast of man,
For God upholds this wonderous plan,
Unwaning in His power!

Years roll apace, and we must wend
To Death's dark portals down,
Through which our fathers did descend,
With warrior, king, and clown:
And all unknown, in darkness deep,
Forgetful of the Spring, they sleep
Until the world's end.

Yes, all must go! – pride stoop thy head –
To mingle in the clay,
Our children o'er our dust will tread,
Our memory pass away,
Till dawns the long expected morn
When men shall spring, as springs the corn,
Out of their dusty bed.

Ye in the dust who long have lain,
Awake, and sing, new-born!
Spring walks abroad upon the plain,
And decks the budding thorn;
O'er ridges green and flowery lea,
Her fresh'ning dews she scatters free,
Or pours the balmy rain.

Ye toiling sons of men, distressed,
    Ye sons of sorrow, cease,
To wander sadly and depressed,
Unknown to hope and peace : –
The Great Divine who all things made
Shall his poor suffering children aid
    And lead them into rest.

Chirnside, April 23, 1858. H.

◇◇◇◇◇◇◇◇

The Emigrant's Longing for Home

I long to be back to my ain countrie,
    And my wee cot hame mid the Lammermoor hills,
For there's nought in this land so dear can be,
    As the breath o' yon moors, and the sound o' their rills.
Long hair-grasses waving wild on the fell,
    And the green rashes bending beside the stream,
Forever in my thoughts by daylight dwell,
    And come to my soul in ilk midnight dream.

Oh could I again wi' our ain folk meet,
    When the heather's in bloom by Kilpalet burn,
Or see once more the mist-wreaths fleet,
    At gloamin, on the hills, by the Dun side cairn.
But weary is the heart in a fremmit land,
    And sair, sair I sigh for my childhood's hame,
Where oft I was led by a father's hand,
    And a kind mother bless'd me, when e'enin' came.

When the wild thyme is red on ilk mossy brae,
    And the bees hum sweet over heights and howes,
And glad roam the herds on the sunny day,
    When before them are feedin' their lambs and yowes.
O then I would be on yon moorlands brown,
    When the knowes are purpled wi' heather-bells;
Or lie midst the waste, when a plaintive soun',
    Soughs through the bent – or sighs in the dells.

It would cheer my heart could I tread once more,
    A' the ferny banks o' the moor-born Dye,
Or the grey sides o' Dirrington clamber o'er,
    Where my fathers roam'd in the days gone by.
From the steep Blyth-edge, fresh the breezes blow,
    Blue-bells bloom sweet by the Trottin Shaw;
And up the Waatch Water's brae I'd go,
    And joy frae ilk bush and stone could draw.

But far, far's my hame – and my heart is sad,
    Though on fancy's wing ay I'm hame-ward borne;
And Oh, my soul it would make right glad,
    To once more up-bind the Lammermoor corn;
And gather once more at the gloamin's fa',
    Round the ingle-side o' my father's cot,
Wi the kind leal hearts – now scatter'd a' –
    Where in life's morn pass'd our peaceful lot.

But I mourn, and lament, and sigh in vain,
    For ae blink more o' my native shiel,
And the hoary old hills, wi' their mist and rain,
    That time to my eyes will no more reveal.
In the old kirk-yard my fathers sleep
    Where the bones o' their son will never be laid,
For here I maun rest in the forest deep,
    Where no kindred dust will be o'er me spread.

The sons o' the hills, in their mauds o' grey,
    Will think never more o' the exile lone,
Forgot, like the dead, who are wrapt in clay,
    I maun here abide till my time is gone.
But my bairns will love this western shore,
    For it is to *them* no alien scene,
And for their sakes I will hope once more,
    And rest in the Power who our guide has been.

Chirnside, June 30, 1858. H.

The Ascension

'Twas forty days, since from the grave, the crucified arose,
The Lord of glory, from the tomb of stillness and repose,
Where in death's adamantine arms the just and righteous lay,
Till dawn'd on earth the glorious morn of his appointed day.

He burst the fetters of the grave, and with triumphant scorn
Broke all the powers of death and hell on that illustrious morn;
The Roman watchers at his tomb, as men in death, lay pale,
And fallen backwards to the ground, in their encasing mail.

The Marys at his sepulchre, did wait at dawning grey,
But he was up at early morn, exulting, and away;
The Saviour rose, and looked on earth, and Satan and his crew,
With open front, ne'er dared again, the combat to renew.

Full forty days he spent below since the thrice hallowed morn
That saw him issue from the tomb – the lately crowned with thorn!
With his disciples oft he met, and with instructions rare
He taught them what henceforth on earth they had to do and bear.

The forty days were gone, and now the Lord must go from hence
And pass into the heavens high, his place of recompense,
And there prepare a place for those resolved to follow on
To bear the cross throughout the world, and reap the martyr's crown.

He led them out, the holy Christ, as far as Bethany,
He led them out – his chosen ones – the men of Galilee:
And wondering at the gracious words that from his lips did flow,
They stood entranced, as men inspired, and could no further go.

They stood, a band of lowly men, the village mount upon,
And in the midst, the Prince of Peace, the son of Mary shone!
And from the well the maidens pass'd, and from the fields around
The labourers came, and pass'd them by with reverence profound.

The sun shone out, and Judah's land in smiling glory lay,
As conscious of the holy one that there stood by the way;
And looking on his followers all, his heart with pity glow'd,
And lifting up his hands on high his blessing there bestow'd.

Departing now from mortal scenes, where he had toil'd and bled,
And wrought the great salvation out, for men by Satan led;
He there beheld the faithful few who would his absence mourn,
Weak and despised, left on the earth to long for his return.

But go he must, the time was set, the father called him home,
And, if he should not go away, the spirit would not come
To strengthen and refresh the flock, on mountain, vale and shore,
The followers of the Lamb of God – the tried in sorrow, sore.
How would they, in this world of strife, temptation, and of guile,
Keep on the course of sanctuary, and separate from the vile;
Renounce the pleasures of the flesh, and mammon's gaudy show,
And onward press towards the prize through peril, pain and woe!

"I leave you in this vale of tears, but man your souls with this, –
The comforter will come to you amidst the wilderness;
Your prayers and supplications true for evermore I'll hear,
And in all time my faithful ones shall to my heart be near.

Go forth then, through this world of woe, and preach the cross alway,
My spirit shall possess your souls and with you ever stay;
Through all the ills and woes of man the gospel star will shine,
And to time's farthest verge shall bear the hope of man divine!"

And now his hands he lifted up, and while the blessing sweet
Flowed from his gracious lips sincere, in majesty complete,
He from their company parted was, and through the air upborne,
He up ascended gloriously, more radiant than morn!

While all intently gazing up, as he ascended high,
A cloud received him from their sight, and they were left to sigh;
But in their ears his blessing rang, and in their bosoms warm,
The love of Christ was glowing there, all ills away to charm.

And forth they went, resolved to go devoted on their way,
And through the world proclaim his love, and life's eternal day
And shall not *we*, with eye of faith, *their* glorious track pursue,
And follow on with confidence that nought can e'er subdue?

How long shall foolish men delight to drink the wells of sin,
The false deceitful, fleeting joys that drug the soul within!
Still with perverted, desperate bent we seek the alluring train,
And though oft proved their hollowness, still seek them o'er again.

O' shun this world's allurements vain – its low pursuits despise,
And soar away with rapt desire, to glory in the skies!
The groveling aims of earth avoid, its fading glories leave,
And seek the fount of heavenly joy, where we no more shall grieve.

To Zion's holy land we'll go – the city of our God,
Where walk in white array, the bless'd, forgot life's weary road;
And singing by life's river pure the praises of the lamb,
We'll rest for ever in his love – no storm to break the calm!

There's sorrow on this earth below, and blighting care awaits
Each child of pale humanity who enters through life's gates;
But looking to the risen Christ who sits at God's right hand,
We'll patient bear the ills of time, and seek the heavenly band.

Chirnside, August, 1858. H.

An Autumn Ode

The spiky rushes browner grow,
The bur-reeds where the waters flow
With darker tips appear.
The willow-herbs still waving tall
With rosy bloom, shall shortly fall,
And frosts their beauty sear.

Still wave, though few, the azure bells,
And eye-bright's bloom, on moorland fells
In speckled beauty fair;
While on the broomy pastoral knowes,
The curly-doddys deck their brows,
And lure the wild bee there.

But soon shall fade the Autumn flowers,
And from the umbrageous forest bowers
The verdure soon decay;
Already o'er our woodland views,
The Autumn tints are dash'd profuse,
And changed from day to day.

The green-tree's foliage, crimson dyed,
Glows beauteous on the forest side,
The elms grow yellow too;
The ash's pale-green leaves drop down
Upon the pathways damp and brown,
Which thickly they bestrew.

The clustered rowans overhead
On yonder ledge grow brightly red,
While brambles creep below,
Whose jetty berries thick emboss
Their stems, that entertwine and cross,
Beside the streamlet's flow.

The ridges now are strip'd and bare,
Where lately waved the barley fair;
And in the furrows green
The partridge brood the fowler shun,
But, hark! before the murderous gun
They whirr across the scene.

The ripening hips on bank and brae
Their brilliant orange tints display,
Ere nipping frost pass o'er;
And haws in rich profusion shed
For winter birds, a feast is spread
From their Creator's store.

The tawny leaves, now fallen and sear,
Tell of the wan declining year,
And point our own decay;
And drooping sad, mid woodland glades,
The songsters see the withering shades,
And pour the mournful lay.

A wailing dirge at evening's close
Tells of the winter's coming woes,
And rustling through the gloom,
The leaves are toss'd and scattered wide,
Or whirled in heaps by forest side,
Where late did roses bloom.

Ah, sad the scene! and cold and hoar –
The flaunting bloom of summer's o'er,
The harvest gladness past;
And Man comes forth like floweret fair,
To flourish in earth's mortal air,
In bloom of beauty cast.

But soon his strength and blossoms fail,
And struck by fell diseases, pale
He falls to rise no more,
And scattered like the autumn leaves
His hapless race, in sorrow grieves
O'er their brief journey sore.

In shrouding mist the landscape lies,
And deep and dreary mourning rise
On evening's sobbing breeze,
Which to me seems some warning given
By spirits, freed from earthly leaven,
To seek from sin release.

We see how all on earth is vain,
How in each joy is flaw or stain,
How thousands pine and mourn,
And frail, as leaves and flowers, we pass,
And wither like the summer grass,
And go, and ne'er return.

Hence may we seek the "better land"
Where by God's river's glorious strand
Life's tree immortal blooms;
Where care or sorrow, toil or woe,
On man no more their shades shall throw;
Or Time its dreary glooms.

Chirnside, October 2, 1858. H.

A Farewell to Lammermoor

Fareweel to the hills, the brown heather hills,
That the steps o' our forefathers bore;
Fareweel to the rills, the sweet mossy rills
That wimple their way to the shore;
And fareweel the dells, the bonny green dells,
And the shielings of old Lammermoor!

O fareweel the knowes, where the purple thyme grows,
And the milk-wort sae blue on the fell;
Fareweel the howes, wi' their lambs and their ewes,
And the cots, where the shepherd-folk dwell;
Fareweel to the Dye, that murmuring vowes,
And ilk rush-shaded rivulet and well.

Fareweel to the Law, and the green broken shaw,
The abode of our race, in the ages of old;
Fareweel to the broom, where the hill breezes blaw,
And the linties sing sweet by the fold, –
We maun part frae them a', ere the autumn-leaves fa',
And wander far off frae the wold.

The hoary old cairn, where in langsyne was laid
The dust o' the warrior, mouldering low,
And the long waving grass, o'er the stones at his head,
In the gale sighing sad, replies to our woe;
And ilk rush-border'd rill, and ilk brae, fern-clad,
We cling to them closer while parting to go.

Ye dear native scenes! on the peaks o' thy hills
The last gleams o' day now are lingering sweet,
The mist o' the gloamin' now rest on thy rills,
And thy hirsels repose on the turf's dewy weet;
And while sleep shuts the breast frae life's troubled ills,
O'er those scenes of my youth I mourn with regret.

Ye leal-hearted herds, wi' your mauds on the lea,
I maun part frae ye a' and be here seen no more,

We will meet ne'er again, in our frank honest glee,
And my heart ne'er was torn wi' sic sorrow before
I face in despair the wild, wide, foaming seas,
And in sadness depart from my dear *Lammermoor*.

June, 1859. H.

◇◇◇◇◇◇◇

The Harvest Concluded

The yellow fields of ripening grain
The reapers' hands have quickly ta'en,
The poor man's hope – the rich man's gain,
Is garner'd well,
And scarce a stook doth now remain
O'er Lauderdale.

O'er the broad Merse, the crop is shorn;
Big, lusty stacks, the yards adorn;
On all the farms is rowth o' corn,
Full stores abound;
And gleaners in the dews o' morn,
Now rake the ground.

Far o'er the stubble-ridges wide
The partridge-brood in coveys hide,
Or where the hips are ripening red,
They bask in dern,
Or burst away with whirring speed,
O'er brake and fern.

For all the genial hours and days
Of summer's sweet, resplendent blaze,
For freshening breeze, and shadowy haze,
We bless Thee Lord –
And heart and tongue most grateful praise
Shall Thee accord!

The teeming harvest of our land,
For all their fruits on Thee depend;
The wheat and barley from Thy hand
Comes forth mature;
And in Thy goodness shall we stand
For ever sure!

The days and scenes of Harvest sweet,
Makes every pulse of pleasure beat,
And waiving fields of golden wheat
Still charm our view,
And every year such scenes we greet
With rapture new!

O may the poor our plenty share,
Nor young or old be pressed with care;
May want and misery be rare
Or land within!
And Peace aye bless our Borders fair
While seasons run!

Chirnside, September 20, 1859. H.

◇◇◇◇◇◇◇

The Rush-Bush

"Green grow the Rashes."

I love the Rush that greenly grows
Where fount or rill serenely flows;
I love the Rush that bending low
Upon the pool its shade doth throw;
On marshy spot, or mossy stank,
The Rush-bush, rising strong and rank,
I love to view when leaves are sear,
And when, through withered hair grass long,
The autumn-winds, a solemn song
Pour forth unto the waning year.

I love the Rush that shades the well
Where once our rustic sires did dwell;
I love the Rush, still fringing sweet
The streams that laved our infant feet;
The Rush-bush green, on burn-side lone,
Calls up the years long, long agone,
    Where wore we cap, and sword, and crown,
And happy wandered in the mead
With mates – long numbered with the dead,
    Whose sun, at early day, went down.

More than the garden's finest flowers,
Than all the wealth of Flora's bowers,
I love the Rush beside the stream,
Green, in the summer's sultry beam;
Or when its verdant days are past,
'Tis shook by autumn's withering blast,
    And strews its wreck upon the burn –
For to my heart 'twill ever be
A living legend, walking free
    The dreams of life's romantic morn.

To me, the Rush will never spring,
A common or a worthless thing;
Its structure, and its fern are plan'd,
Like all God's works, by matchless hand,
And shows an art that's all divine,
In power, and wisdom, and design;
    And men shall ever love to see,
The rushes plet by infant hands,
To verdant sceptres, wreaths, and bands,
    While seasons pass o'er wood and lea.

The yellow leaves now falling, fade –
Rave on, ye winds, through dell and glade;
The Rushes now, are brown and sere,
Rave on, ye winds, your dirges drear;
But yet through withered rush and reed,
Your moaning voice may fancies feed,

And wake the spirits of old days: –
The infant bands! I see them met,
To weave the green, rush, coronet,
Beneath Romances mellow rays, –
And many a joyous, simple scene appears
That bless'd my early, happy years,
By mossy braes and rivulets clear,
Where pass'd like morning mist, our fears
And nature's arms enclasped us, dear.

October 7, 1859. H.

◇◇◇◇◇◇◇◇

St. Abbs

What boundless power did Thee command,
A barrier to protect the land,
And 'gainst the tempest-tossed brine,
Rear'd up this strong opposing line?
God sways the blast, and rides sublime
O'er the vast deep, – and in all time
Hath said – while billows rage, and tempests blow, –
"Here shalt thou stop, nor further go."

Piled rude and rough, thy ramparts high,
Lour forward to the sea and sky,
While heaving waves with foamy crest,
Are dash'd to spray upon thy breast;
And every splintered cliff and scaur,
Have stood the ocean's ceaseless war,
For centuries of bygone years,
And still unshaken stands and bears;
The east wind fierce, and roaring surge,
Have uttered here their wailing dirge,
While the wild scream of drowning men,
Have echoed through the lonely glen.

Since from the troubled, restless main,
Fair Ebbs's skiff did shelter gain,
Upon this rocky, rugged shore,
What changes have this world pass'd o'er!
What generations of our race,
Have pass'd away and left no trace,
Of all their thoughts, and words, and wiles,
Their laboured monuments and piles,
Have mouldered like themselves away!

And smiling morn or stormy day,
Will never from oblivion's cell,
Rouse them to view the ocean's swell,
Till all these rocks shall melt with fire,
And nature in the flames expire;
But till that morn of terror rise,
Here shall be heard the sea-fowls' cries;
Here on the rocks the flowers shall bloom,
Here still shall wave the thistle's plume,
And wild-bees pass from flower to flower,
And wild moors glisten in the shower,
Of summer's sweet refreshing rain,
And head-land stern, and level plain,
And cove, and dell, and placid lake,
To nature's votary still will make
Sweet pictures to allure his eye,
And cheer his heart 'neath cloud and sky.
The fleecy mists in autumn's breeze,
Will pass along the moory leas,
And shroud St. Ebbs's brow and side,
While dashing deep below, the tide
Will foam along old Lumsden shore,
And by Fastcastle's ruin hoar;
While through the piled clouds of the west,
The sun descends o'er mountain crest,
And throws his red departing gleam,
O'er rush-clad howe and rippling stream.

Perhaps St. Abbs, I'll ne'er again,
Sit on thy brow, and view the main,
Wild clashing at thy feet below,
While fowls unnumbered come and go;
And sweeping winds their path-way trace
Along the ocean's changing face;
But in my mind's recesses still,
Thy bleak stern scene shall pictured dwell,
And while I consciousness retain,
Sweet thought of thee will still remain.

Chirnside, November 23, 1859. H.

◇◇◇◇◇◇◇◇

Solitude

O, for some place of solitude, where I could be alone,
In Nature's silent green retreats, by moss-encrusted stone,
Deep in the wood, low in the dell, beside the purling rill,
Below the hoary hawthorn bush, where all is sweet and still.

Where pale, the scented wood-riff blooms upon the mossy brae,
And stately fox-glove's spotted bells, their lovely bloom display,
Where on the green, untrodden bank, the cuckoo-clover springs,
And where the blue geranium blows, and blithe the linnet sings,

The birks, amidst the hazel bowers, their fragrance sweet diffuse,
And from the dark sloe-thicket near, the merle plies his muse;
Then glows the heart with ecstacy, beneath the hawthorn hoar,
And nature fills her votary's soul with all her pleasing lore.

Rejoice, rejoice, O gentle heart! lone-sitting in the wood,
For every impulse Nature gives to thee is fraught with good,
From birds, and flowers, and budding trees a balm of healing flows,
And beauty's in the tinniest moss, as well as in the rose.

The voice of God is heard among the rustling of the trees,
And Nature's dulcet melodies will true hearts ever please;
In shady groves, beside the stream, a "still small voice" we hear –
"Peruse the volume at your feet – the Great Supreme is near!"

While bumming past, in happy mood, the honey-laden bee,
Home to its cell in swiftness flies – a worker bright and free,
It tells of God's almighty power, and attributes benign,
While chirping praise on sunny bank the crickets all combine.

While falls the dew on barren wastes, or on the fertile plain,
While murmurs on the mountain rill a poet-soothing strain,
The chequered pathway in the wood the poet's feet will tread,
And teachings from blest Nature's hand will ever be his meed.

'Tis not because I hate mankind, I seek the forest shade,
Nor that because my heart's impure, of them I am afraid,
But there's a sweet congenial charm that draws my soul away,
From all their bustle, pride, and guile, in solitude to stay.

So shy in worldly aims I've been, so poor in worldly show,
I shrink from all the crowded ways in which the million go:
Alone! alone! I'd be alone, remote in bowery dell,
For in the shades of solitude, I would for ever dwell.

There's no abiding on this earth no stable joy is here,
But while I journey on the way, I would have quiet cheer;
Far from ambition's course I'd keep without regret or pain,
And through the lowly vale of life walk on in even strain.
The votaries of trade and wealth may at me flout and jeer,
And for my choice of solitude, my name in pieces tear,
But let me walk as I have done, and do what good I can,
And I'm content unmarked to be – though still in soul a man!

December 28, 1859. H.

Up to the Moors

Now, I will to the hills ascend, the old brown heathy hills,
I love to breathe their bracing air, I love to hear their rills;
I love to hear the mountain bee in gladness booming bye,
The bleating of the ewes is sweet on thyme-clad hillocks high.

I love to see the purple bloom across the moorlands spread,
The heather-blooms o' Lammermoor, I love, I love to tread;
I love to wander by the marsh that plough has never torn,
I love to see the rush-tufts wave where ne'er has wav'd the corn.

The yellow club moss creeping low by mound and mossy stone,
The blae-berry on the sunny brae, are sweet to look upon;
Fair on the dark deep well below is pictured *Ordweil* steep,
And through the *Strait-loup's* pass above the roaring waters leap.

From bosky brae and shady dell, the morning mist's withdrawn,
And on the Law, and lone *Ellba's* the glory of the dawn;
Then on, and on, I'll wander on, the *Whare-burn* sweetly flows,
And green's the bower o' *Shannabank* where blooms the wild-
wood rose.

Up on the bank the birch tree waves and sheds its fragrance sweet,
While bramble, lithe, and fox-glove tall cling round its mossy feet;
The veiled nuns that wont to tread *St. Bathans* shady vale,
In dust have lain for ages long, and gone to bless or bale;

We'll tread the paths which once they trod, by wood and water's
side,
And wander o'er *Straphunton* braes, where moor-born streamlets
glide:
The cloud-shades pass o'er *Godscroft* lea, once cheer'd with poets'
strain –
And fleeting, like life's pleasures flee, as transient and as vain.

Still on we go, through heath and brake, to *Monynut* we hie,
And muse along by *Laikyshiel* beneath the summer sky;
Up to the moors! the far wild moors, and roam the desert free,
The voice of Nature calls me there – the linnet and the bee.

The wilding flowers that gem the waste, the wild winds sighing low,
Recall the dreams of bygone days, and soothe me as I go;
The gushing spring and lapsing rill in soft refreshing sound,
Fall sweetly on the listening ear, and bless the desert ground;

A spirit in the desert dwells, and works in bud and flower,
And through the wreathing mist we hail, His wonder-working power;
Each tiny insect, bird, and bee, doth in His smile rejoice,
And all the hills doth sing His praise with soul-enlivening voice.

Up to the moors! the ancient cairn, where waves the hair-grass slim,
Shall be my seat, till shades of eve make moor and mountain dim;
Up to the moors! the ceaseless hum of Nature's voice I hear,
To Lammermoor my heart is drawn – her hills for ever dear!

April 7, 1860. H

To the Memory of JOHN YOUNGER, Shoemaker, St. Boswells, Who died of Paralysis, on Tuesday, June 19, 1860

Like common men the prophets die,
And mingled in one haven lie;
Like common men the poets yield
To death upon life's battle field;
Like common men they pass from earth,
No claims allowed of higher birth;
They pass away! the self-same road
By mean and noble must be trode;
They pass away – the sons of song,
Unnoted midst this worldly throng;
They pass away – and where is he
That ere bewails their destiny?

A few days past my friend was here,
And *now* he's reached another sphere,
Whose powerful mind and busy brain,
Oft wove the sweet congenial strain;
From straits of age, from pain and woe,
And all that haunts our life below,
Where want's gaunt shadows cannot come,
He's entered to the glorious home.

St. Boswell's Bard! Now hast thou gained
Life's river clear, that ne'er was stained
By earthly dross, or aught impure
That we in this low state endure;
From all life's sins and troubles freed
In deep repose now rests that head,
Where cares and toils no more molest,
Or sorrow break his endless rest.

A truer, kinder, better heart,
Ne'er in this world had a part;
Nor nobler soul, or clearer head,
E'er down life's path in honour sped;
What though in toils obscure his years
Passed by, with all their hopes and fears;
Yet with a manly soul and keen,
He trode this many-chequered scene,
While musing deep on man's high claims –
His nature, destiny, and aims;
And pouring forth his fervent lays
In Nature's breast, in Nature's praise –
He midst her glory sunk to rest,
And at his Father's high behest,
His earthly harp dropt in the dust,
And followed on with child-like trust,
Through the dark gate that leads to day,
And glories ne'er to pass away.

Dear *Younger*! we thy name revere –
A Poet, and a Man sincere,
Of strong intent – a worker true,
That social hearts around thee drew,
Of different aspect, mein, and creed,
For better men ne'er walked on Tweed;
And Border men, of distant times,
Shall kindle at thy stirring rhymes,
And drop a tear above thy sod,
From age to age, in thanks to God,
Who reared thee up – a Bard and Sage,
Our hopes to brighten – griefs assuage,
And in life's thorny paths infuse,
Still sweeter flowers, and balmier dews,
And chase from toiling men, afar,
Despair's thick mists, and lurid star.

Chirnside, June 25, 1860. H.

Hearts Easily Won are Easily Lost

A constant glowing heat is better than a blaze;
A heart that truly loves ne'er in its light decays;
A fire that burns low will last till night is by,
While conflagration's red will in the darkness die;
Great heats are over soon and leave but ashes black,
A heart consumed with love doth meikle wisdom lack –
Give me the constant soul that Truth may countersign,
But hearts most easily won – you will as easily tyne.

The fickle wavering mind, aye veering here and there,
Now in a lofty mood, now down in deep despair,
Is not for world's wear – is not for man's delight,
But glances meteor-like, while darker glooms the night;
Love founded on esteem, on worth, and dignitie,
Will live though fortune frown, and till life's well is dry;
A tender, mild regard – a faithful love be mine –
For hearts most easily won – you will as easily tyne.

The toils, and cares, and griefs that darken life's career,
Are gilded by the love that's changeless and sincere,
A type of faded sweets that bless the ever leal,
In yon far happy land that death can but reveal;
Through dangers darkest course let us unfaltering bend,
While on a truth-fast breast we truly can depend;
But proud, vain, flaunting ones will never reach that line,
For hearts most easily won – you will as easily tyne.

The tinsel gauds that deck false fashion's slavish crew,
Can only dazzle those to virtue never true,
But hearts that cope with life, and nobly strive to rise,
Will all their gew-gaws vain, as worthless trifles prize,
Time's gross deceitful joys shall tempt us not to stray,
From out our quiet path, far from ambition's sway;
And resting in our loves, we'll neither fret nor pine,
For hearts most easily won – you will as easily tyne.

July 16, 1860. H.

Sonnets on Viewing my Native Stream

Stream of life's early morn! still gliding freshly on
Through the green bur-reeds passing softly sweet,
Where 'neath the yellow Iris, hid from summer heat,
Lies the red-spotted trout, beside the slimy stone;
Sweet through the rushes and the waving plume
Of the tall meadow-queen, the gentle breezes bloom,
And waken many thoughts of years long passed away;
For here I used to roam, and watch the wild bees' flight.
From bloom to bloom of fragrant clover gay;
There I have plucked the blae-berry, and the lotus bright,
Or midst yon fern-tufts for a while been hid,
When the tawned reapers toiled above the brae –
O could I once call back those scenes so cherished,
And have one glance again of all their fair array!

Perished and gone those actors of the past,
Or only fleeting by in dim and misty dreams,
Half shadow and half light. Beside the rippling streams,
Now waves the barley ridge, and over all is cast
The bright enlivening gleams that make the landscape glad,
But there's a glory gone – a charm for ever fled
From these green mossy banks we trod in boyhood's morn:
Where is the reverend sire who often wandered here?
The tender mother, where? Gone from this nether sphere,
And all the little band, that sported by the corn,
Are scattered far and wide – and the old home-stead dear,
Where the old patriot-virtues can grow out-worn,
Is levelled with the ground – But O thou streamlet clear,
Thy soft sad murmurs soothe a heart that is forlorn!

The wildness of thy meads bedecked by Nature's hand,
With all the bloomy sweets, to children consecrate,
Have yielded to the sway of culture's prideful state,
And bog and moss are gone, where flowed the fountain strand;
And even the ancient crooks that formed thy wildered way,
Man's hands have tampered with, and now are all,
With thy lone verdant nooks, beneath his niggard thrall;

But with a gladder heart I'd seen thy waters stray,
As when upon thy pools, I launched my tiny fleet,
Or sat amidst the herbage, listening to the call
Of craik and partridge – rural sounds most sweet –
O will they ne'er come back, those scenes departed long?
O will I hear no more the ancient harvest song?
And will I never more with my old comrades meet?

Chirnside, July 18, 1860 H.

◇◇◇◇◇◇◇◇

Our Hedge Side Flowers

In our common paths and ways –
Where is much to please and praise –
Flowery plots, and grassy nooks,
Mossy banks and silvery brooks,
Meet us as we roam about,
All our country lanes throughout.
In the garden's cultured bounds,
In the fertile fields and grounds,
Much of wealth and beauty lies,
But I love and greatly prize
All the flowers that wildly spring,
Free-gifts of Nature's offering, –
Works of most consummate grace,
Brightening every desert place,
Showing forth the power and love
Of the Almighty One above.

Every day we love to see
All the charms of bush and tree,
All the wild flowers, blooming sweet.
Spurned as weeds by vulgar feet: –
In the hedge the purple vetches,
Round the twigs their tendrils catches,
Clinging, trailing o'er the bushes
Of the hawthorn, furse, or rushes,

Giving grace to road-side fences,
And delight to travellers' senses.
There's the clover, red and white,
Blooming for the bees' delight,
Enamelling the swairded ground,
And diffusing fragrance round,
While the yellow crow-toes cover
Blooming patches, 'midst the clover,
The curly-doddy's azure flower,
Nodding in the broomy bower.
Blue-bells bright, on slender stalk,
Waving o'er the grassy balk;
There the mill-foil's varied hues
In clustered beauty, bloom profuse,
Mingled with the tall knop-weed,
With its crown of lovely red,
And the rest-harrow, creeping low,
On the bank makes pleasant show,
With the yellow agrimony,
Smelling sweet, as new made honey.

Now the blue geranium blooms
Brighter blue than Persian looms
Ere displayed in any mart;
Brighter too than hands of art
Ere could picture or display,
St. John's wort blooms beside the way;
Meadow-sweets, with snow-white plume,
Throwing forth a fine perfume,
O'er the ditches, bend and meet,
With the hair-grass, slim and neat,
Willow-herbs so bloomy red,
O'er the rills their blossoms shed,
While the bur-reeds, cool and green,
Deck for us a lovely scene,
Where we love to wander lone,
By the waters lapsing on;
On the mossy, ledgy brae,
Where we love so well to stray;

Blossoms, yellow in the heat,
Ladies'-bed-straw, smelling sweet;
There is too, the fragrant thyme,
Lovely in our northern clime,
Blushing red, on moor and waste,
Meet posy for the hands of taste,
And Roses, blooming, blushing fair,
Forms of beauty everywhere,
By the banks and hedges blow,
And o'er their verdure glory throw:
In native grace – in nature's care,
All these blooms their season share.
They are "teachers sent from God",
To instruct us on the road,
They are sent to soothe and cheer;
And our home-stead to endear;
Paths, without their floral light,
Would be scenes of gloom and blight;
They, in all their beauty dress'd,
Are with Wisdom's seal impress'd;
Every bud, and leaf and flower,
Tell of goodness and of power;
Every blossom speaks to man,
Of the great Creator's plan
His creatures' gladness to enhance,
As they through this life advance,
Telling of His love and care
To all who breathe the ambient air;
Wooing men, with forms divine,
Blooming in the summer shine,
In His grace and love to rest,
Who this wondrous globe hath dress'd.
With such matchless skill and art
That fills with joy the trusting heart.

Chirnside, September 1, 1860. H.

September – A Sonnet

A sun-gleam on the distant hills! And sweet
The mellow glow enwraps the Merse's plain,
Where fields of golden wheat, in Autumn's ripening stain,
The traveller's pleased, delighted senses meet;
The reaper-bands pour forth a gladsome strain,
And on the rustling ridge bind up the fruitful grain,
While up the furrow's edge the gleaners' little feet
Wander from stook to stook, and merry tales repeat:
With joyous, grateful heart the barley sheaves I see
Upraised along the slopes, in many a row complete,
While on the purple moors the happy toiling bee,
Gathers the latest sweets 'gainst winter's bitter sleet
O great, benignant God, save now our fruits mature
That with abundance blessed, may be both rich and poor.

Chirnside, September 11, 1860. H.

◇◇◇◇◇◇◇

Lines on hearing Garibaldi compared with William Wallace

Yes, Garibaldi, thou art great! But greater far
Was our great patriot of this northern land
The leal, the glorious Wallace, who, with single hand,
Withstood the Southern tyrants, and their war;
Illustrious he rose, and formed a faithful band
From the true-hearted *commons* – while's country's *chiefs* a-scaur
Stood back, aloof, or under the base command
Of Edward, tore their mothers' vitals – and did mar
The march of Liberty – and did meanly right withstand:
Yes, Garibaldi, thou art great! – and numerous hearts
Shall bless thy name – for many good and true
Are with thee, and thy great deserts
Shall float on grateful tongues, Italia through;
But Garibaldi! never measured, be thy meed,
With our great Wallace, who of Patriots all, was head!

March on, renowned chief! true, brave, humane,
Trample down tyranny with thy resistless tread;
The despots power shall at thy coming wane,
And vile oppressors shrink with horror dread
Before thy face – nations shall kindle up
To hail thy advent – Venice of old renown,
Will rise once more, and drink of Freedom's cup;
Hungary's oppressed race will rise, and Kossuth come
To lead his ardent brothers 'gainst the oppressor's crown,
Resolved to make their land of true free men, the home;
Go on, illustrious chief! and make Italia free,
Nor heed the banded anarchs, who may scowl on thee
Thy name shall stand entwined with matchless William Tell,
And other names who fought for Freedom well,
But still our "Wallace wight" *will ever bear the bell*!

Chirnside, October 22, 1860. H.

◇◇◇◇◇◇◇◇

Ann of Blanerne

On thy bonny green banks, O Blanerne,
How softly the gloamin'-shades fa',
And sweet flows the river a-down thy green vale,
While the birds to their coverts withdraw:
But Anna, the dear one's not there.

She'll never come back to the bonny green braes,
Where the heart of her laddie was won;
For far, far away in the deeps of the sea,
The beloved of his bosom sleeps lone;
And he mourns for his Ann evermore!

O dear to the heart o' the yellow-haired boy
Was Anna, the sweet and the true,
And sore bleeds the heart that was widowed so soon,
To wander the wide world through,
Without the sweet smile o' his Ann.

In a far, foreign isle, with no friend to console,
He sighs for his own native shore,
And sad is his heart for the 'loved of his soul,
And how dreary the scene lies before!
While he ne'er can forget his dear Ann.

On the bonny green banks of Blanerne
I'll ne'er look with gladness again,
Since she, the sweet bride, in her life's early morn,
Has gone down to the deeps o' the main,
And will never revisit us more!

She has gone to her rest – to the land of the leal;
Let her memory be hallowed and sweet:
While the primrose shall bloom on the braes o' Blanerne,
And her name there the breezes repeat,
In a strain ever plaintive and low.

Bewail not the dead who have gone to their rest,
Bewail not the maid who was dear;
But let bitter tears flow for the exile forlorn,
Whose bosom the anguish must bear,
As he thinks on past joys wi' his Ann!

November 3, 1860. H.

The Ever-Green Polypody

In bleak December's gloom is there no beam of light
To cheer the soul, when heat and verdure's past?
Is there no beauteous gem, when the cold freezing blast
Sweeps howling by, augmenting winter's blight,
To move the heart with feelings of delight?
Oh yes – even then are lines of beauty cast
Upon this earth, which sweetly do contrast
With all the barren bleakness of the winter's might: –
Along the muddy path, I trode but yesterday,
From out a mossy wall[1] in thousand fronds of green
The Polypody sprung, hanging each graceful spray,
Over the crusted stones, and crevices between;
On height and hollow 'round the rain descended fast,
And gathering wreaths of mist the landscape did invest,
Yet in the darkening day with sweet surprise I viewed
The long, low, ancient wall, with moss and fern bestrewed.
Perhaps those pleasing forms were passed unheeded by
When fair flowers blushed profuse beneath the summer's sky;
But now, when winter frowns, their beauties more appear,
And show more brightly green when dark declines the year –
So in man's prosperous day, eclipsed by fashion's power,
Patience and mercy shrink before the gilded show,
And come not forth until affliction's hour
Sweep all vain phantoms from our path below:
Wealth's false allurements fade, and faith points out to sight
The green celestial tree, that death shall never blight,

Chirnside, December 3, 1860. H.

[1] *Between Hammerhall and the Piper's-house, Blanerne.*

Evening

The evening comes – her mantle grey
On all the hills is spread;
Meek silence at the close of day,
Comes forth with gentle tread
Along each green and grassy way,
And o'er each dewy mead.

The dew descends – a silent power,
God's sweet refreshing dew
Sprinkles each leaf and drooping flower,
Their vigour to renew,
And o'er the wild blooms of the moor,
Sheds its bright pearls too.

How gladly now we close the door
'Gainst worldly noise and care,
And grateful, count the mercies o'er,
We through the past did share,
And from our Father's bounteous store,
Hope still for daily fare.

How welcome is the night's repose,
How sweet the rest it brings,
When toiling men their labours close,
And care his burden flings
Down, where the wretched and their woes
Sleep under slumber's wings!

O blessed sleep! like silent dew
Steal down on weary eyes,
Like balm on aching hearts, renew
The joys we once did prize,
And in thy dreams, grant us a view
Of coming Paradise!

Sleep calmly ye, whose hearts are sore,
While craiks harp 'mong the corn,
And peaceful nights for evermore
Precede each happy morn –
Since "God's beloved," not heretofore,
Nor now are left forlorn.

Chirnside, June 24, 1861. H.

◇◇◇◇◇◇◇◇

Lines Addressed to a Family Circle

O bright young band of smiling ones! unscathed yet with care,
Your brows unclouded still remain, no trace of sorrow there,
You see no trouble in your way, no time of coming woe,
But sport like lambs in flowery fields, as on ye prattling go.

The toilsome way is yet untried – the miry path of life,
The scramble for existence here, the bustle, and the strife,
The hidden pits and dangers dark, the tangled mazes there,
You see them not, you fear them not, and all your views are fair.

You know not now the weariness, the fever, and the fret,
The hopes deferred, the obstacles that on your course await,
The crookednesss of worldly minds, duplicity, and guile,
That you must all encounter here amidst your day of toil.

You know not now the slanders vile that will your names assail,
The jeering scorn that meets your path, if e'er your feet shall fail,
Remorse, regret, and vexing thoughts that will your souls dismay,
When from your own, or others' faults, ye falter on the way.

The sons of pride, malign and base, will cast their withering blight,
Upon your quiet and humble course, while holding to the right,
But firmly still your standard grasp, though trodden to the clay –
You'll rise again, and toil again, and God will be your stay!

I love to see your glistening eyes, your laughter ringing free
Is sweet to hear at evening hour when sporting in your glee,
I love to mark the rosy hue on lip and cheek that glow,
And hear the tones of each young voice that thrills my bosom so!

The tresses fair, the gait and air, of each and all the band,
The simple joys of innocence that move each heart and hand!
And all your prattling artless ways are cheering to my soul,
Amidst the daily cares of life, as time doth onward roll.

O could you nestle always thus in your parental home,
Like birds beneath the brooding wing, and never distant roam;
But go you must, and sad I'll be, and severed here and there,
Where will you rest your aching heads – your weary hearts, O where?

How will you bear the bitter storms that round your heads shall blow,
While passing o'er the wastes of life, amidst the drifting snow?
When far away from home and friends, with hearts depressed and sore,
You muse upon life's early joys – departed ever more!

But there's a hope, a brighter hope than e'er from earth has sprung,
That faithful ones shall happy be, and evermore be young;
There is a heritage beyond life's dark and troubled sea,
A heritage of lasting bliss, where sorrow cannot be.

July, 1861. H.

Foulden Hagg

To Foulden Hagg I love to go,
I love to trace its grassy lane,
When birchen bowers their odours throw,
And cushets in their shade complain:
I love to hear the laden bee
Boom o'er the tangled wilderness;
The feathery ferns I love to see,
And yellow mosses love to press,
That o'er the knowes in beauty creep
Where timid hares in frolic haunt,
Where hermit wrens there covert keep,
And linnets through the summer chant.
Give me an hour to wander there,
Give me to drink at Nature's fount,
Give me to taste her balmy fare,
And in my verse her charms recount!
On mossy couch let me recline,
And listen to her soothing strain,
And let the rich 'midst grandeur dine,
But let me Nature's wisdom gain,
And I for gold will ne'er repine.
Sweet are the voices of the woods,
The many voices of the trees,
The harping crickets' merry moods,
The sighing of the summer breeze,
Ah, sweeter far than worldly crowds,
And fitter far the soul to please!

To Foulden Hagg I love to go,
And have my heart to Poesy trained,
Where rushes green and willows grow,
And rasps and brambles unrestrained.
Then to the Hagg once more I'll stroll,
And lonely muse its bowers among,
For while I on life's courses roll,
My heart will thrill to Nature's song!

August, 1861. H.

April

How sweet our lovely primroses
Begem yon mossy brae,
Where soft the springlet oozes
    Beneath the hawthorn grey!
There, too, the pilewort yellow
    Unfolds its lovely breast,
Where hangs, above, the willow,
    In buds o' siller drest.

The sloe's dark boughs are laden
    With blooms of snowy white;
And the violet! – modest maiden –
    Peeps out in azure dight:
The April breeze caresses
    The wind flower's blossom fair,
And the birch tree's fragrant tresses
    Wave in the balmy air.

From day to day, the roses
    Expanding more and more,
In fresher green discloses
    The dell's perennial store:
The mosses by the fountains
    In greener patches rise,
And on the heathy mountains
    Is heard the peewits cries.

Go forth then, child of sorrow,
    And trace the bosky dean,
Thy heart will solace borrow
    From nature's gladsome green;
The voice of waters pouring,
    The soaring laverock's strain,
Will chase thy glooms o'er louring
    And make thee hope again.

The colt's-foot by the river,
  Bursting in leafless bloom,
Pass it not careless ever,
  Though void of sweet perfume;
Nor pass wilt thou the gowans
  In heedless humour by –
The great Creator made them
  To show his wisdom high.

His goodness still renews them –
  Earth's fairest buds and flowers,
O'er bank and cliff he strews them,
  To glad the April hours.
In lone, remote recesses,
  Their matchless beauties rise,
God on them sheds his blessings,
  Though men their forms despise.

Mad after mammon's treasures,
  And grubbing deep for gold,
Men leave sweet nature's pleasures,
  And are to lucre sold:
But nature! breathe thy spirit
  Upon our souls for aye!
And wealth we shall inherit
  That never knows decay.

Far o'er the moors and mosses,
  And desert regions wild,
The sun-blink often crosses –
  A gladdening radiance mild:
So midst life's stormy weather,
  Hope's brightening bow appears,
And courage new we gather
  'Midst April's smiles and tears.

Chirnside, April 25, 1862. H.

Lines on the Death of Mr John U—

The barley is ripe, the oat fields are yellow,
And gone from the village the swift flying swallow;
The harvest is come – Hope's flag is unfurled,
And God's bounty is scattered wide over the world:

Come forth now, ye reapers, and "thrust in the sickle",
Cut down the ripe wheat, for the weather is fickle;
Bind up the full sheaves – hear the oats how they rustle
In the bright gleaming sun, where the harvest-men bustle.

But alas for the day! our home-stead's in sorrow,
And no reaper will come to our fields on the morrow;
For our head's-man is gone far away from the Border,
No more to call forth all his reapers in order.

No shouting in harvest, but wailing and weeping –
'Mong the maids there's no gladness as they go to the reaping;
The old men are sad – the women are mourning,
For they'll never more see their master's returning.

The Bereaved – who will cheer her when *he* is departed?
Oh meek Man of sorrows! shield her broken-hearted –
When her help is cut off be her comfort, and cheer her,
In her day of distress, be Thou, Lord, ever near her!

He was peaceful and kind, and no tyranous driver –
His way it was gentle – no brawler, no striver;
Without show or pretension, his course it was even –
And now he has gone where his joy is unriven.

Called away when the ridges where white for the sickle;
Called away when his help was needed right meikle;
From his labours he rests, with the vast countless numbers,
That have gone on before to their long silent slumbers.

Chirnside, September 11, 1862. H.

Lines on seeing Spring's First Daisy

Lovely little Daisy,
Hast thou come again?
Blooming by the furrows,
Where the snow hath lain,
Opening thy fair bosom
To the lord of day,
While the lark above thee
Pours his fervid lay.

Lovely little Daisy,
Tipt with beauty's hue!
Oft my heart hath blessed thee,
Shining in the dew
Infant hands have called thee
Ere Homer was a boy,
And they, through all the ages,
Have made of thee a joy.

Lovely little Daisy,
Nursling of the field!
Our Father here hath sent thee
A ray of hope to yield.
The winds of March may chide thee,
Beside the springing corn,
But still thou wilt not yield thee
Unto their blistering scorn.

Lovely little Daisy,
Cheerer of the soul!
Shall storms of care depress us,
And energies control?
We hold the faith that surely
We're in our Father's hand,
And He who formed the daisy,
Our lot in love hath planned.

Lovely little Daisy,
        Sparkling here and there,
Our lonely paths are gladdened
        With thy blossoms fair,
Thou art on the mountains,
        Thou art in the glen,
Preaching of God's mercy
        To the sons of men.

Lovely little Daisy,
        Harbinger of Spring!
The dew of morn is on thee,
        The lark thy praises sing,
I cannot choose but love thee,
        Sweet love of life's young day!
Thou bringest up the dear ones,
        Who long have passed away.

Lovely little Daisy,
        Star of moor and waste!
Come forth ye darling fair ones,
        With innocency graced,
And mark the blooming Daisies,
        And thank the God of Flowers,
And render grateful praises
        For Spring's delicious hours!

Chirnside, March 1864. H.

Scenes of Boyhood; and Other Poems (Facsimile)

Apology for Quality

We must apologise for the quality of some of the pages of this facsimile reproduction of the original 1840 edition of *Scenes of Boyhood.*

This book is very scarce. At the time of writing, we know of only one copy, at present held by the Scottish Border Archive in Hawick. They do not have the means of electronically scanning to a sufficiently high standard and are unable to allow it to leave their premises, so we have had to work from a photocopy.

As must be expected of a book printed at that time, with what looks like old and worn type on paper of variable quality, some problems of legibility will arise. It is hoped that these will not too seriously spoil the reader's enjoyment.

THE

SCENES OF BOYHOOD;

AND OTHER POEMS.

BY GEORGE HENDERSON,

SURGEON

BERWICK:

PRINTED BY C. RICHARDSON, WESTERN LANE.

1840.

PREFATORY EPISTLE

TO A FRIEND.

MY DEAR SIR,

An old writer says, "such physicians as I have marked to be good practitioners do all piddle somewhat in the art of versifying, and raise up their contemplation very high, and their verses are not of any rare excellence." * What truth there is in this I am not prepared to say; but it is well known that we have an illustrious list of men who were great poets, and good physicians—Blackmore, Garth, Akenside, Armstrong, Darwin; and though last, not least, the excellent Moir of Musselburgh. At all events, there is no reason why a man of poetical aspirations should not be a good physician. I am inclined to think it a very favourable sign in a man of medicine—and a sort of guarantee that his professional duties will be performed with diligence

* English Translation of "Huarte's Examen de Ingenio."

iv

and humanity. It will, at any rate, greatly contribute to his happiness—for there is nothing more conducive to a man's enjoyment than for him to be possessed of poetical talents and feelings—it invests all things with the hue of romance and beauty—and in the creations of his fancy, he finds a source of pleasure more enchanting than can be found in all the glitter and luxury of the most prosperous fortune.

You know that I have, for several years past, devoted part of my leisure time to the cultivation of Rythme; and in the principal piece which goes to make up this little volume, I here present you with the fruit of a week's musing, with frequent interruptions. None can be more sensible than I am of its many imperfections; but having no time to abridge or alter it, you must receive it as it is.

Part of my object in the following Poem was, to show the evils and injustice of Monopolies in Agriculture. Large farms, like every other extensive accumulations of property, I have always considered as very injurious to the well-being of society at large. The land is not better cultivated when under the management of *one* wealthy individual, than when possessed by *ten* men of small capital—witness the small farms of Belgium: and small farmers may be as intelligent, persevering, and industrious, as our great gentlemen-farmers, who make such a flourish in

V

the present day. I indeed think small farmers the most respectable of the two. "The more elegance and luxury among the farmers," says Robert Burns, "I always observe, in equal proportion, the rudeness and stupidity of the peasantry. This remark I have made all over the Lothians, Merse, Roxburgh, &c.;" I would therefore denounce unsparingly the plan of throwing many small farms into one large possession. It destroys the most valuable class of our peasantry—and I never pass a large farm, but I involuntarily say to myself—"How many happy homesteads may be made out of this extensive domain, where now only one powerful tenant rules and revels?" Let landlords consider what misery they create to thousands, by dispersing their small tenantry, and throwing down their ancient dwellings. Neither their lands nor their rentals are improved by it—and what though a few men of large capital may flourish by this method, it cannot compensate for the loss of those who have been ousted to make way for these great men. No!

"Ill fares the land, to hastening ills a prey,
Where wealth accumulates, *and men decay*.
Princes or lords may flourish or may fade,
A breath can make them, as a breath has made;
But a *bold peasantry*, their country's pride,
When once destroyed, can never be supplied."

You will perhaps object to me that I have been needlessly severe on the wealthy and titled classes vi

of society. Take a survey of the world, and say whether I have overstepped the bounds of truth or justice, in my hurried picture of the aristocracy or their minions, or of those who ape them in feelings, principles, and conduct. But far be from me, the uncharitableness to include *all* in these sweeping charges and denunciations; there are glorious, noble, magnanimous exceptions—men who make their wealth a fountain of blessings—a source of infinite good to their fellow-creatures, and a well of happiness and peace to their own souls: for we are only happy, in proportion to the happiness which we procure to others. Wealth is far from being a blessing to any man, unless he makes it an instrument of good for the community in which he dwells. Indeed it cannot otherwise be. Man is an immortal being, destined hereafter to a state of endless bliss or misery—and is it not an absurdity to suppose that *an immortal soul* can find happiness or peace in the accumulation, and niggardly grasping of money? Or how can a man find peace in spending it upon his grovelling lusts and appetites?—in loading himself with "thick clay"—bartering away his peace, his everlasting peace, for "filthy lucre's" sake, and burying himself deep in gross, sensual, animal pleasures? Believe it never!

I trust you will excuse me for what I have said respecting our Established Priesthood. You know my opinion on this point long ago. To endow

vii

churches is only to tempt the cupidity of worldly and ambitious men, who enter into the ministry for " a piece of bread." To give a clergyman an income of three or four hundred pounds a-year, is only enabling him to keep pace with the rank of the gentry in his neighbourhood—and is throwing him into a whirlpool of fashion, sensualism, and degeneracy, which is most inimical to the exercise of virtue or piety. Some say that such endowments are necessary to render the clergy *respectable* in the eyes of the world, and to ensure the reverence of their people. Respectability indeed! Reverence indeed! That minister will not fail to be respectable, nor will he want the reverence and love of his people, though very poor, if he zealously, and with single-mindedness, pursues the steps of his Lord and Saviour Jesus Christ, who was " meek and lowly"—the companion of fishermen and mechanics! But alas! how unlike their Lord and Master are many of the smooth, gentlemanly priests of the present day?—a set of mere fashionable men of the world, and bitter partisans, whose *worth* consists in anything but zeal and activity in their Master's service!

" The Saviour came not with a gaudy show,
Nor was his kingdom of the world below;
The crown he wore was of the pointed thorn;
In purple he was crucified, not born.
They that contend for place, and high degree,
Are not *his* sons, but sons of Zebedee."

viii

Having all along considered the working classes, (in which I include small farmers,) to be the genuine strength and power of the country—no wonder that my sympathies are all on their side. I cannot look upon the proud, tyrannical, and overbearing lordlings of our land, without indignation and disgust: and they who follow in their wake, and aspire to ape their manners and their ways, are worse still. " Aristocracy soon to be effaced from the world, gives place to the sordid and ephemeral middle class, without root or vigour. The populace alone, that populace *which works*, still preserves some character, and some virtues. Tremble, if it should ever learn its power."* The artificial grades and villanous *castes* or distinctions of society have ever gained little of my concern. I consider them a perversion of nature, and I can never be brought to see any superior worth or respectability in a man because he is rich, titled, or powerful, unless he possesses some far more ennobling attributes which quite outshine his riches or his titles. But the world calculates the worth of a man by his money and possessions —not by his talents, piety, or virtue. Here is a man worth £6,000 a-year—he is a great man, say the Mammonites. Well: he has £6,000 a-year—a great sum!—but wealth or property is no part of *the man*. Twenty pounds a year will procure

* Lady Esther Stanhope.

ix

any rational being meat, drink, and clothing. The rest will only serve to keep up a glare and a flourish, and a pomp of attendance. I would reverse the matter thus. Here is a man who has £600 a-year—he gives away *four hundred pounds* annually of this money, to relieve the miseries and distresses of his fellow-creatures—to spread intelligence—to promote the practice of piety—to further civil and religious liberty—to spread the gospel in Heathen lands, &c. Now I would say that this man was *worth four hundred pounds* a-year. For unless a man makes his wealth the means of doing good, it becomes an absolute curse to him, even in this world, and makes him a very *worthless* person indeed. To make our wealth conducive only to our selfish ends—and the aggrandisement of our own families, is to turn it from its legitimate purpose. It is a talent which must be accounted for. Men are only *stewards* of their wealth, and they cannot do with it as they choose, without incurring the Owner's displeasure. But I am no *leveller*—such a principle I detest, as being opposed to the nature of things in general, and to the nature of man in particular. Men cannot be *equal* in point of worldly property—but I claim for *all* the citizens of a free state *equality* in point of privilege, whether of a religious or political kind. There ought to be no favoured sect—no pensioned aristocracy—no hereditary legislators—*no taxes on bread*, or on free trade—no unscrip-

x

tural alliance of Church and State, in any well regulated Government. But even in point of *circumstances*, the inequality between the rich and the poor, in our country, is far too enormous—the chasm is far too wide between the *privileged* and the working classes, ever to work well—and the rich and the titled are always too ready to look down on the poor with a cruel, ungenerous, and jealous eye; and perhaps the poor are too apt to regard the rich with envious and malignant feelings.

Let the working classes endeavour, with all their might, to get rid of their too frequent, gross and degrading habits—such as drinking of intoxicating liquors—the greatest bane of all self-respect and happiness. Let them try to inspire themselves by a higher tone of morals; and strive to enlighten and ennoble their minds, and purify their hearts, by knowledge, virtue, and truth. Yet there is in *labour itself*, a dreadful obstacle to the amelioration of the human race. What man after ten or twelve hours of severe and exhausting toil, day after day, can have any heart or power to improve his intellectual or moral nature? Such a condition is almost hopeless—seeing that this incessant toil is barely sufficient to procure the necessaries of life—and such men can have little taste for anything but some sensual or brutal excitement. The first point then for the improvement of the working classes, ought to be a restriction of the hours of labour—say to *eight hours a day*—and this would be quite sufficient for all essential worldly purposes, both to the employers and employed, were men not such decided votaries of Mammon,—and determined to make *gain* at all hazards,—eating up one another, and throwing down one another, not by a just or honourable competition, but by an unprincipled and ferocious *cannibalism*, most disgusting to behold! Indeed, till such a change in the hours of labour takes place, I would despair of improving, in any essential point, the great mass of mankind. Even Religion can have little real or practical influence upon men's hearts—toiled to the utmost stretch of their physical capabilities, and bound on the rack of perpetual care for themselves and their children. But of this no more here.

In the following pages, I claim for myself no elevated walk in the regions of Poetry. I am content to be thought of as one who delights to wander about the skirts of the Parnassian hill—and I shall not be disappointed to see other walking in a higher sphere, and basking in the sunshine of popular favour: yet the lowly violet shows not unlovely beneath the shade of the peerless rose, or the stately fox-glove. My theme is local, and I have no wish that my name should extend beyond the locality of which I sing. The scene of the succeeding Poem is principally laid in the south eastern part of the parish of *Buncle*, in the Merse, where I spent the first twelve years of my existence.

It was once my intention to have made the Notes much more copious—but the prescribed limits of the volume have induced me to abridge them very materially. As they are, I hope they will not be uninteresting.

I am,

My dear Sir,

Yours sincerely,

G. HENDERSON.

CHIRNSIDE, JAN. 3, 1840

SCENES OF BOYHOOD.

Where'er our feet have wandered hill and dale,
O'er Lothian's plain, or Yarrow's classic vale; (*a*)
Or where by Leader's haughs we view'd old *Rymer's* tower;
Or spent in Dryburgh's shade the evening hour;
Or pluck'd the bonny broom on pastoral Cowdenknows,
Where shepherd-maiden milk'd her father's ewes;
Or down Tweedside have lingered even and morn,
And sat entranc'd beneath the trysting-thorn;
Or stroll'd, at noon, down Eske's romantic glen,
And view'd the ancient caves of haunted Hawthorn-
den; (*b*)
Or where Lochmaben rises on the plain,
We lonely saw the Bruce's fair domain;
Or stood beside the grave of Robert Burns,
With saddened heart " midst obelisks and urns;" (*c*)
Or where the Nith pours down her waters clear,
We look'd on Elliesland, (*d*) once to the muses dear;
Or, where o'er Cumnock's plains we sad did stray,
When wild the snow-flake drifted o'er the way;
Or bleaker still, where Dunsyre hill doth rise,
We view'd, with sinking heart, the stormy skies;
Or where sweet Airth (*e*) beside the Forth appears,
We've wandered with our friend, whom we have lost for
years;
Nor there, nor by Dunedin's turrets grey,
Such glorious scenes could e'er mine eyes survey

B

14

As those which I beheld, when from my father's door
I stood and gazed our Border vallies o'er.

These native scenes still charm our eye and heart,
And still a genial influence to our soul impart;
Though viewed each day, they still each day delight,
Deck'd in their summer green, or robed in winter's
white—
And still their charms will fill our bosom's core,
Till life's vain toils and sorrows are no more.

Upon the north, old Buncle's (f) hills extend,
Once clad in forest green, from end to end,
Where erst the wild deer bounded through the glade,
Or from the fairy-haunted rill, beneath the shade,
Drank the cool waters, while the sultry day
Beam'd on the sloping banks with ardent ray;
And there the powerful Stuart's mellow horn,
Was heard afar upon the summer's morn,
Rousing his vassals to the hunting gay;
Or readier still, to the wild Border fray—
When bloody feuds embroil'd the country round,
And slaughtered peasants strew'd their native ground.
Those days of sylvan game that on our forests shone,
Have left no traces on the mountain lone:
The days of Border broils, and pillage too, are o'er,
And rude moss-troopers scour our plains no more:
But marks of older times upon the hill are seen,
Where oft, with musings strange, we've trac'd the
trenches green;
There the old Britons camped on the height,
Ere Roman eagles northward took their flight;

15

And there I've lain upon the hill-top grey,
'Mong heather-bells, and mountain berries blae,
Gazing with lightsome heart o'er hill and plain ;
Cheviot's blue mountains, and the marled main ;
The fertile Merse, with shady hedge and tree,
The fields of waving corn, and grassy lea ;
The smoking hamlet and the ruin hoar ;
The gay, green slopes, with cattle sprinkled o'er ;
The sparkling river, and the sun-lit mead ;
The wind-mill tower, and far-seen farm-stead ;
The ancient churches, and their graveyards lone,
Where lie the wrecks of ages, past and gone ;
The halls and groves, where lords and ladies dwell,
The lowly cots that please my fancy well,
Where sons of labour light their fires at even,
And worship God, who hath all blessings given.
Yet small's the portion which the poor enjoy
Of toil-earned gains, which all their days employ ;
From year to year, their strength is spent and torn,
That wealth may revel in her pride and scorn—
Their toil upholds the world's glare and show,
Yet small's the pittance which of wealth they know ;
And grudged is still the little that they get,
For Mammon's children ne'er had pity yet.

Pine not, ye sons of toil, though scorn'd and poor—
Though ground to dust, your labours still endure ;
Your Father hears your groanings, and will not despise
Your offerings meet, though worthless in men's eyes ;
In his good time, your tyrants shall be tamed,
And of oppression's trade be made at last ashamed;
Let useful lore your leisure hours engage,
And study, for yourselves, the sacred, hallowed page,

16

That ye may know the truth, and to the truth adhere,
Nor like the wavering reed, with every whisper, veer.
Walk firm in virtue's path, nor swerve to vice's side,
Nor basely yield to foul corruption's tide;
An onward course, 'gainst pride and fashion steer;
And sternly brave, keep all your heart-springs clear;
Ne'er meanly crouch before the great man's tread;
Nor fawn, like spaniels, for a piece of bread;
Sneak not, like slaves, for lord or lady's hire,
Nor lick the feet which tread you in the mire;
Erect your souls, like men who think and feel,
Nor be, like beasts of burden, driven with goads of steel.

But turn we to our theme, and view our native vale,
Where Nature still sends forth the primrose pale;
And daisies pied upon the emerald lea—
When April comes with tear-drops in her e'e.
Yes! o'er these scenes my fancy ever broods,
And views them all with various thoughts and moods:—
How sweet in ancient days those wooded hills would be,
When heroes strode through dell and forest free;
When *Wallace wight, (g)* with his brave followers all,
Ranged through the woods, that look'd o'er Buncle's wall;
And haply, laid his head beneath the oaken shade,
The God-protected one, of mortal ne'er afraid!
And slumbered there, on moss and fern green,
While night's cold dew fell on his cheek serene.
O Wallace! Wallace!—ne'er a name like thine
Can make my bosom thrill with feelings so divine!
Great Patriot Chief! who set old Scotland free,
Would I had strode our mountain glens with thee;
And by thy side, midst peril, blood, and strife,
For Scotland's weal laid down my wayward life;

17

For nobler heart did ne'er old Scotland see,
Than glowed within the breast of him of Elderslie!
Who trode undaunted honour's bright career,
And in the battle's brunt his heart ne'er shook with fear.
Ten thousand curses on their memories rest,
Their tombs be ne'er with flowers and laurels drest!—
The *nobles* of those times, who thwarted all his care,
To free his native land from vile oppressors' snare!—
The dastard souls who 'gainst the Hero strove,
And sunk in death the Patriot's quenchless love!
Eternal infamy shall cloud their fame,
And sink them deep in everlasting shame.
Such spirits still in Scotia's vallies lower,
Who flaunt in wealth and pride, and lord it o'er the poor:
Such are they all, who own the Tory race,
And for their selfish ends do power and riches chase!

How sweet upon those woods,—now weeded all away,—
The sun's last gleams at evening would decay;
Slanting with golden light through foilage dense and green,
While on the shaded turf the flocks reposed serene;
On pastoral Lammermuir sunk down the summer dew,
And twinkling cottage-lights gleam'd on the traveller's view.

Now Fancy turn, to yon old hoary trees,
That stand, a lonely group, shook by the autumnal breeze;
There stood our cottage 'neath the flickering shade,
Skirted by garden snug in rose and mint arrayed;
In sunny nook the hives in order stood,
With busy inmates storing up their food;

18

The raspberry there, and currants flourish'd sweet,
And gooseberry too—for boys a famous treat!
Byre, shed, and barn, behind the ha' were plac'd,
And many a grassy plot the sheltered hamlet grac'd,
Where thrifty goodwife bleach'd her linens white,
And boys and girls played there, like fairies light;
A row of thatch'd cots stood by the croft-land green,
Where lads and lasses by the doors were seen,
When gloamin grey bedimm'd the distant vale,
Listening to rustic song, or fairy tale;
While the loud laugh rung through the merry band,
And the wild harping craik, called from the clover land:
But darker night came o'er the ridgy lea,
And chill the breeze sighed through the aged tree:
Then 'round the hearth the cottagers withdrew,
Where hoary sires gave all monitions due;
And now the Holy Book is from the crevice ta'en,
And praise and prayer, in simple fervent strain,
Is uttered forth beside the cottage fire,
By man and maiden, matron, child and sire;
When worship's o'er and supper at an end,
All to their rest the rustic inmates bend;
And there in sweet repose their wearied bodies lie,
Till the lark calls them up their daily tasks to ply.

But there no more the evening psalm we'll hear,
Nor song nor glee shall the soft breezes bear:—
The green is gone—the garden bower's away,
And all our homestead levelled with the clay:
No more our feet will tread the cottage green,
Nor there again will cot or ha' be seen;
Still stand the trees, like ancient veterans there,
And wild the blast moans through the branches bare;

But there no more shall be what once hath been;
For fell Monop'ly triumphs o'er the scene;
And bloated grows, like hemlock by the wall,
The monster vile, that makes our country fall!

Down the lone burn-side, at the evening hour,
The Autumn mist dim o'er the banks doth lower;
Dark through the wreaths that roll above the brook,
For the departed ones, with bleeding heart, I look:—
A sister's form, who in her early years
Left this cold world, with all its hopes and fears,
Methought I saw, lingering beside the brae,
But yesternight, as lone I pass'd that way;
And in her hand she led a lovely child,
Who pointed to the stream, and like a seraph smiled:—
For that sweet child my woe-fraught heart did yearn,
For oh! she seem'd my own, who left us here to mourn
Only a month agone:—but in a moment then
The vision faded in the mist and rain,
And as I o'er the vale with sorrowing bosom pass'd,
I heard sad voices mingling in the blast. *

There by yon marshy spot that skirts the way,
The self-destroyer rests, 'neath sedges grey;
Spurn'd from the churchyard, where her kindred sleep,
And thrust, like dog to rot, by foul ditch deep.
The stunted willows o'er her lone grave sigh,
And withered rushes on the cold turf lie:—
With terror oft we've shunn'd the haunted spot
At twilight grey—and scampered to the cot,
Lest the pale suicide should start to light,
When all alone we pass'd with dire affright. *(h)*

* This description is from a dream of the Author.

20

Still, as I pass those scenes of school-boy days,—
The well-known spots that saw our childish plays,—
I feel a sad regret for pleasures past and gone,
And look, with heavy heart, on all those places lone:—
The grassy lane, where wild flowers blossomed sweet,
Where 'mong the sand we ran with shoeless feet;
The primrose banks that bound our native rill,
Where flags, and sedge, and rushes flourish still;
The ferny brae, where little emmets dwell,
And where we sought the wild bees' mossy cell;
There, too, the blae-berry blossom'd on the steep,
And the gay lintwhite sung with pathos deep;
There the lone wagtail watch'd beside the stream,
Or skimm'd along the pool, like to a passing gleam:
There in the purling brook we sought the speckled
trout,
Or climb'd the haw-tree for its clustering fruit;
And where the grey wall bounds the public way,
A wild rose-bush doth still its bloom display;
From it the scarlet-hips we pluck'd in long past years,
And still to me that bush the scene endears;
And where the ragged whins, with blossoms gay,
Cheer'd the wild waste, in summer's sunny day;
There with the herd-boy on the bank we've lain,
Or rear'd the turf-shiel on the furzy plain;
Where, sheltered from the blast, we conn'd some ancient
lay,
Of glorious battles won—or Flodden's mournful day.

Down the brown foot-path, shaded by the corn,
The rustic maiden tripp'd at summer morn,
(While swallows skimmed with rapid wing the croft,
And laverocks sung in misty air aloft—)

21

To fill her pitcher at the fountain clear,
That flowed, above the burn, from year to year;
There sitting by the margin of the bonny well,
I've heard her plaintive melodies in rapture swell:
She sung the strains of Caledonia sweet,
Wild mingling in the vale with the young lambkin's
bleat—
Then with full vessel hied her up the slope,
Dashing the dew-drops from the wild flower's top—
Gone is the footpath, and the gushing spring,
And there no more the merry maidens sing:
The green well-strand is gone, its waters drain'd away,
And there no more shall cottage lovers stray,
When the dim twilight spreads her grateful veil,
And steaming mists yon low green banks assail.
Changes are busy with our world and race,
And selfish men still push us from our place;
Seasons revolve to blight our prospects here,
And all our cherish'd flowers relentless sear.
We go—as went our fathers of the vanish'd years,
To the dark grave—where there's no hopes or fears.
On yon green slope, where ewes and lambkins feed,
Me, by the hand, my father oft did lead
To view his flock, wide scattered on the lea,
When mild the evening sun shone over land and sea;
Then *Help** ran scampering by our dewy path,
As on we wandered up the lonely strath;
The startled partridge on her pinions borne,
Whirrs quick away, o'er brake and waving corn;
Help with keen bark fast follows on her track,
But follows far behind—and panting, soon comes back.

* The name of the shepherd dog.

22

Down in yon hollow, which the banks enfold,
We pluck'd the marsh-flowers by the fountain cold;
Or pull'd the rushes from their watery bed,
To plait the belt, and helmet for our head.
There, too, we waded through the streamlet deep;
Or laid the lint in dark moss-pool to steep;
Or there, in gladness, coil'd the scented hay,
While nature all was smiling, bright, and gay;
The tedded swaths we toss'd, in boyish glee,
With blooming maid of roguish twinkling e'e;
There at the mossy well we quench'd our thirst at noon
And toil'd till evening o'er the mead came down:—
That bog is drain'd by modern art and care,
And all is changed since we disported there.
I love the uncultured spot, where Nature revels free,
Some place left sacred to the flower and bee—
But few such spots now near our home remain,
All must be torn, to add unto our gain:
The marsh and *common* now must feel the share,
And culture's hand be busy everywhere:
Our land doth flourish, say the great and wise—
Improvement's march makes still the markets rise;
The rich men richer grow, and roll about at ease,
And bloated luxury doth her fancy please;
The pampered lordling struts his gilded days,
And all his wealth, in insolence, displays—
He boasts his horse, his chariot, and his wh—re,
And rides in triumph o'er the wondering poor;
All privilege he claims, and right, and law,
And labouring men of him must stand in awe!
He spurns the poor with insult and with scorn—
For him, and such as him, the poor were born!

23

Drive on ye rich!—and revel, hunt, and feast,
Nourish your hearts, and worship still the Beast—
Cry—" Church-and-State!"—and pour libations out
To Mammon, Bacchus, and their fleshly rout!—
Yet far are ye from peace, though riches overflow,
And men grow weary of your empty show.
Yet flourish on, ye proud! ye rich! and high!
Lay field to field, and heap to heap apply.
Our land doth flourish!—and hath prospects fair,
Though poor men weep, and struggle in despair!
In hopeless toil they grind from hour to hour,
And pine in woe, crush'd under tyrant power.
Still down and down the labouring classes fall—
Poor serfs and slaves, they're bound in Tory thrall!
Yet still our land doth flourish more and more,
And grandeur decks the rich from shore to shore;
The poor increase, and still their comforts fly,
Dear is their bread, and clamorous children cry
For food and clothing, shivering in the cold,
While sons of Mammon grasp their glittering gold:—
" Still flourishes our land!" say all the great and wise,
And what to them are poor men's groans and cries!
Poor labour droops, and famish'd thousands mourn,
And fell distress hath millions crush'd and torn;
In penury's cells how many pine and die!—
But who for this e'er heaves the pitying sigh!
Fashion and pride must flaunt and glitter still,
And luxury riot in his lust at will:
Shall not the rich enjoy their boundless stores,
And frown the unfortunate from their guarded doors?
Their wealth's their own, and who dare claim a part?
Shall they not use *their own* as *self* directs each heart?—

24

Keep down the poor!—and grind them day by day,
Work them like brutes, and give them scanty pay!
Such is the tyrant's cry—the rich man's creed,
And State-paid Priests "give scripture for the deed."
So will it be, till o'er the bloated mass
Destruction's wheel, like whirlwind fierce, shall pass:
Let wealth's proud children revel in their lust,
And in their gold place all their hope and trust!—
But evil days are hastening on with speed,
When they in vain for mercy's aid shall plead;
The ground is failing underneath their feet,
For power abused shall retribution meet;
The earth is heaving with volcanos dire,
And drench'd in blood and tears, Monop'ly shall expire!

But yet, in future times, shall dawn the hour,
When selfish men shall wither in their power;
When o'er the world benevolence shall reign,
And vice shall die, with her fell offspring, pain:
The rich, with liberal hand, shall then bestow
Their stores on want, and soothe the bed of woe:
Then toil shall reap the fields, in harvest gay,
And no oppressor frown his joys away;
The poor shall eat, in their abundance glad,
And on their heads God's blessings ay be shed;
No tyrants then shall rule, with iron hand,
Nor grasp at large domains of cultured land;
For all shall then be full, and all content
With that good portion which the Lord hath sent;
None shall usurp another's right—nor with deceit
Man with his brother man, or neighbour meet;
Pretenders base, their guilty heads shall hide;
And smooth hypocrisy, and cursed pride,

Shall skulk in corners, and be shunn'd by all,
And gilded fashion by their side shall fall :—
Truth, peace, and liberty shall rule the earth,
And love preside by every sacred hearth ;
Then lust shall rage, and misery pine no more,
And slander's foul, polluted reign be o'er :—
Ye wheels of time ! roll on your rapid race,
And bring the glorious days, the age of grace !
When man with man, like sons of God, shall dwell,
And hallowed, happy years time's future annals tell:
No evil passions then this earth shall blast,
Nor sons of Belial to their revels haste ;
But sweet sincerity with men shall 'bide,
And Christian purity o'er all preside.

But let us call our wandering fancy back,
To trace the scenes of boyhood's vanish'd track—
Beside the cairn, where still yon mound appears,
Oft have we sauntered in our early years ;
'Round the huge stones, where lay the slaughtered dead,
A group of happy elves, we laughing sped ;
Or on the cairn we sat in thoughtful mood,
And mus'd on battle-fields, and conflict rude ;
When through the vista of long vanish'd days,
We saw the fires of painted warriors blaze ;
And on yon banks saw fierce contending bands
Meet in the strife, and strew the uncultur'd lands
With warriors slain—while *Draedan's (i)* mossy rill,
Ran, stain'd with blood, of dead men on the hill:—
Gone is the cairn, where slept the warriors grey—
The long-piled monument of a forgotten day ;
But still there stands the ancient Druid stone,
Upon whose hoary top we oft have sat alone :—

26

There may it stand for ages yet to be,
As relic of the past, 'twill still be dear to me!

By yon tall hedge, where now the coveys bask,
I've seen the reaper ply his weary task;
And there, behind the band, I've bound the mellow corn,
In the glad opening years of life's romantic morn:
There sun-brown'd gleaners *(k)* picked the scatter'd ears
Among the stooks, and had of man no fears;
With smiling look, the master stood beside
Old withered age, and childhood side by side;
Nor grudged, with niggard heart, their hoarded store,
The more they got his heart rejoiced the more!
Where yon blue-bells and curly-doddies bloom
On the fair knowe, amid the waving broom,
There I have sported with the gleesome band,
And heard their glad shouts echoing o'er the land;
Blithe, on the ridgy field, the harvest-day wore by—
Yet glad we saw the day-star shut his eye:
When weary, down the path, we homeward took our way,
And saw the vesper-star shine through the twilight grey:
Songs of the ancient days rose on the gloamin still,
And plaintive rural sounds floated along the hill.

How happy was that day when won our kirn was there,
When barn-yards were full, and stubble-ridges bare!
When calm and bright September suns did shine,
And mellow'd all the fruits, which glowed like rubies fine
When nut-brown ale, and savoury viands were set
On the full board, where merry reapers met;
In social glee, the hours of night flew past,
While fallen leaves were whirled before the blast.
The goodman clears his anxious brow, and there
Master and servants in the revels share.

27

No pride or state the rustic scene confounds,
But undisguised delight the happy group surrounds—
While moonbeams pale the dim seen valleys light,
And there the wreaths of mist lie cold and white all night.

Where countless reeds once clothed yon narrow vale,
Their feathery heads wild streaming in the gale—
There lay the Myre, *(l)* with moss-pools dark and deep,
Round whose black margins foul toads lov'd to creep:
The wild grey willows waving there you'd see,
Their silvery blossoms opening to the bee;
There red marsh cinque-foil, and the buck-bean grew,
And hoary cannach waving in the view;
The yellow marigold long flourish'd there,
And purple orchis—Flora's offerings fair:
The pale-flower'd cresses o'er the water spread,
And broad green flags with graceful drooping head:
There lit, at night, by vapours foul and dank,
The faithless meteor glimmer'd by the bank,
The 'nighted traveller from his course to lure,
And, 'wilder'd, lead him from the pathway sure;
Some cottage-light he deems the wandering ray,
And follows, in its track, still more and more astray.
For, fated ne'er that vale he now must pass,
But plunging, hopeless, in the deep morass,
Down, down he sinks, 'mong putrid plants and mud,
No more, alas! to rise from that dark flood:
His ghost, they say, at evening hour is seen,
Pale, wan, and drooping, by the rushes green—
Through the white mist, with shrieks, it flits away,
Leaving the lated traveller in sad dismay.

Sweet came the winter evenings dark and long,
Made light and cheerful with the tale and song;

28

Up the wide chimney went the flickering blaze,
Cheering the rustic group with its enlivening rays;
Around the hearth the little children bask,
And there the school-boy cons his morning task;
The father eyes with joy his little urchin's skill,
As he with rare devices all his slate doth fill:
The matron knits the hose, or plies the spinning-wheel,
While the young rustic maid prepares the evening meal;
There in the nook the amorous ploughman swain,
Looks on the blooming lass, with bosom fain,
And sweet stolen glances pass between the twain!
And by the bourtree, on the barn-yard wall,
This night they'll meet, though rain and sleet should fall.
There too, within the ha', the way-worn beggar sits,
With woful heart he sighs and smiles by fits;
While on the children's pranks he casts a wistful gaze,
And thinks with anguish on his early days;
When he, like them, sat by his father's knee,
And claim'd a mother's love, for ever fond and free.
But now for him is lit no hall or home,
And scorn'd and old, he through the world doth roam.
How few regard the homeless wanderer's way,
The lonely, weary outcasts, going still astray!
Houseless and ragged, through the land they go,
Of hope bereft, and worn with want and woe;
Hated and shunn'd by earth's proud busy race,
Who spurn them daily from their dwelling-place;
Sore is their hearts—and far all comfort flies,
And in the grave their only refuge lies!
Yet there are wanderers ever prowling by,
Who wallow deep in vice's filthy stye;
In foulest infamy their nights are spent,
And stain'd with every crime, of which they ne'er repent;

29

With tales of feign'd distress they hall and cot invade—
Deceit and villainy their daily trade!
Yet these demand our love and pity too,
Brothers they are, though dyed in darkest hue;
And wretched sons of vice, sunk in the lowest scale,
Must not be cast where charity doth fail:
To want and sorrow, let thy bounty flow,
And still " forget their vices in their woe!"

Thus pass'd the evenings in the farmer's hall,
While winter o'er the fields cast his cold snowy pall;
And from the eaves depending, long and clear,
The glittering icicles in the moonbeams peer;
Down the hedge-side slow trips the timorous hare,
And a low moaning sound sighs o'er the stubbles bare;
While drifted heaps obstruct the public way,
And frozen brooks glide softly by the brae;
There, on the morn, the merry boys shall slide
Careering on the stream, in noisy glee and pride;
While on the bank the fairy frost-work see,
And hoary cranneuch clothe the willow tree!

Long have those scenes been left for care and woe,
And scattered wide, we sad and cheerless go
O'er the rough waste that leads us to the tomb,
While on our path falls sorrow's dusky gloom:
False friends depart when comes our evil day,
And leave us struggling in the miry way;
Yet heart or hope shall fail us never here,
As down we wander through each varied year:
Let friends forsake, and foes their arrows cast,
Our souls are unsubdued, and ready for the blast;
Let slander pour her venom on our head,
Her foulest vapours we shall never dread!

30

Prepared for scorn, and penury, and pain,
Alike we feel earth's hate and favour vain:
Cast down we may be, but despair we scorn,
And still we look for joy's eternal morn;
We know that here no resting-place is ours,
And false is grandeur's smile, and pleasure's bowers;
Like forest leaves we drop and fade away,
And Time's swift stream no mortal power can stay:—
Stretch then our views beyond this changing scene,
To yon bright land, where Eden's bowers are green!
Where Sin, and Death, and Woe—those horrid three,
Shall enter never, to pollute Life's tree!

Though such our thoughts, we still look back to view,
The sweet lone scene, where first our boyhood grew;
Our parents then in vigour flourish'd there,
And pleasures many was their earthly share;—
But *now*, alas! at life's frail, evening hour,
Their hopes are crush'd, and sorrows on them pour.
O God! protect them as their days decline,
And smoothe the path, that they may never pine,
Till the last trial is past, and they are ever Thine!

Nor less remember'd is the path remote,
Which to the school we travers'd from our cot;
Oft careless, there we loitered by the way,
To pluck the flowers, or chase the insects gay;
'Midst the wild bracken, and the meadow's-queen,
We've rang'd the dell—a truant band unseen;
Or 'mong the whins, with yellow blossoms drest,
We sought the lintwhite's and the yorlin's nest;
Or climb'd the braes the liquorice knots to dig;
Or chas'd the peesweep o'er the brairded rig;

31

Or scal'd the trees to harry rooks and daws;
Or roam'd the dean to gather hips and haws;
Or by yon banks we lingered night and morn,
To hook the minnows from the wimpling burn;
And where the ancient tower in ruins red, *(m)*
'Mong yon tall trees is by their branches hid,
We paused, with awe, the fallen dome to view,
And thought on days of old, when Earls there withdrew:
O'er the green mounds that skirt the castle wall,
Oft have we scampered at the evening's fall;
Or trac'd the moat that hemm'd the tower around,
Till the long shadows darkened o'er the ground;
There deeds of blood, and martial feats were done,
When these old walls were often lost and won
In the wild Border times of turmoil and dismay,
While banners waved above the noisy fray.
Down by the burn-side, where the alders grow,
Trains of fair ladies there might haply go
To pluck the daisies in the lonely dean,
Or golden pilewort on yon sloping green;
There, mailed knights have stalk'd across the glade,
Arm'd with the glittering spear and sparkling blade;
And there, at night, the roving bands have met,
When flower and grass with heavy dew were wet,
To march across the Tweed, the border dales to scour,
And drive their booty to this northern bower:—
Long, long the actors in those scenes of dread,
Have mouldered low among the countless dead;
And here the revel, and the minstrel's strain,
Shall ne'er be heard by lords or knights again;
The hemlock sad, now blossoms in the hall,
And nettles wave above the desolate wall!

32

Nor will we e'er forget, while memory holds her sway,
The haunted village of the olden day, *(n)*
Where witches met their orgies to perform,
And work the charm to raise the furious storm,
That corn might be destroyed, and ships sunk on the sea,
Or murder done, by some old blasted tree!—
There oft we met, with peers now scattered wide—
(Some smile in fortune's lap—some the dark grave doth
hide;
Some pine in want, and wake to toil and pain,
And some are sighing for their homes in vain)—
To con our tasks, beneath the master's care,
Or mingle in the sports that had the largest share
Of all our hearts, when we were learners there:
Here at the football match with keen delight,
We push'd and drew—and followed in its flight
The ball, now here, now there—now sent along the way,
And hail'd beside the burn, with loud huzza;
Here, too, the shinty's favourite game we plied,
And struck the *nurr* with boyish glee and pride;—
Those sports are past—those merry actors fled!
And oft since then has many a bosom bled,
Which knew no sorrow in those early days,
Now weary winding through life's various ways:
Still oft we pass the bourtree-shaded way,
Where with our comrades young we met to play—
Or, by the brook, we linger yet to view
The scenes where long our school-boy pleasures grew!

Where yon old trees high crown the fertile height,
And the long scattered village rises on the sight;
Thither we went in boyhood's careless day,
When cold November swept the leaves away,

33

To mingle in the fair, whose annual sports and glee
To youths and maidens brought a jubilee:
In prospect bright its merry scenes arise
With magic splendour glittering in their eyes;
And when the long-expected day dawn'd in the east,
Crowds to the *Cross-hill* flock'd, as to a feast;
Where crames, and stalls, and shining wares were spread,
And blithesome faces shewed that hearts were glad;
There comrades met—and lovers fond and true;
And "drouthy neighbours" sat till they were fu':
The day went down o'er shows and pastimes rare,
And sounds of gladness filled the midnight air;
The music and the dance o'er youthful hearts preside,
And revelry flows on with an impetuous tide:—
Sweet is that village with its shady trees,
Its cottage gardens sheltered from the breeze,
Its low-roofed domes where men of virtue dwell,
And hardy toil wards penury from his cell;
Sweet is that church, and crowded churchyard green,
Where lie the dead in slumbers most serene;
The glare and turmoil of earth's *living* race,
Can ne'er disturb their lowly dwelling-place;
And naught can break their dreamless, long repose,
Till the last awful morn seal time's eventful close!
Yes! sweet's our village for its homely scenes,
Its scattered homesteads, and its sloping greens;
But sweeter far for distant views it yields
Of woods and waters, lawns, and cultur'd fields;
There deck'd in beauty, the rich Merse doth lie—
A glorious landscape, spread before the eye!
And far blue hills, and chequer'd valleys rare,
Point out our Border land—a land most fair;

34

Where tale and song still linger by the brooks,
And shepherds wander by green pastoral nooks—
Let pilgrims stray o'er classic lands at will,
No fairer scenes they'll view, than those from *Chirnside* hill. *(o)*

To yon green bowers, beyond the Eye's clear tide,
Where forests once in all their leafy pride
Clothed the steep hill-side, and the dingle lone,
In musing mood, we oft have happy gone
To pass the day beneath the sylvan shade,
Where in the dean our couch of fern we made;
Or sat beside the fox-glove's spotted bell,
Our bosoms fraught with wild poetic spell:
There too we've stroll'd with damsels young and fair,
When ripe September mellowed all the air,
To range the woods, and pull the clusters down
From hazel spray, that bank and brae doth crown:—
Sweet was the day, and merry was the band,
When with young friends I rang'd the forest land,
By Renton fair, or Houndwood's pleasant site,
For contemplation form'd or love's delight!
Through glades obscure, and wild-wood mossy dells.
We wandered free, and drank of fairy wells;
Where o'er the rock the rowan's clusters red,
And tufts of lady-fern were sweetly spread;
But there we'll range the bosky dell no more—
Friends are estrang'd—and I the change deplore.

Down the steep bank that o'er Shawbraes doth rise,
We've wander'd oft, 'neath summer's azure skies,
To bathe our bodies in the pure soft stream,
While through the alder boughs a mellow gleam

35

Of sunlight fair fell on the glassy pool,
And flowery margin of the river cool;
There too, beneath the tree, we pored o'er Cowper's lays,
While coo'd the cushet-dove along the shaded braes;
The tassled birch hung o'er our mossy seat,
And blooming thorn, so odorous and so sweet;
The honeysuckle twined its tendrils there,
And sweet wild-rose shed perfume on the air;
Up the long vale is heard the cuckoo's note,
And o'er the uplands far the mellow sound doth float;
Through all the woods the birds in concert vie,
While sweet the shaded water murmur'd softly by.
Let wealth around us shower, or grandeur deck our line;
Let fame illume our path, or glory on us shine;
Let us traverse the globe, from Shetland to the Cape,
And o'er each land and clime our varied fortune shape;
Yet still this truth shall on our bosom press,
Whether we walk in joy or languish in distress—
Where'er our lot is cast, where'er our feet may stray,
No scenes can please our heart like those of boyhood's day,
And which we ne'er forget, till mingled in the clay.

NOTES.

NOTE A.

Yarrow's classic vale.] The vale of *Yarrow* has been long famous in song. "There is something," says Chambers, "highly *peculiar* in Yarrow. There is more than natural silence on *those hills*, and more than ordinary melancholy in the sound of *that* stream." "Sweet *Leader haughs*" have been long celebrated in one of the finest ballads in our language: on these haughs, near Earlston, stands the ruins of *Thomas the Rymer's* tower,—"Learmont's high and ancient hall,"—where dwelt the famous *prophet* and poet of that name. The shades of *Dryburgh* will long be visited by thousands of pilgrims, who will flock together there to look upon the resting-place of Scotland's most renowned minstrel—and the famed *Cowdenknowes* will continue to be visited by the lovers of song, as long as Leader flows to Tweed.

"There grew the broom, the bonny bonny broom,
The broom o' the Cowdenknowes;
And sweetly there the lassie sang,
I' the bught milking the ewes."

NOTE B.

Haunted Hawthornden.] On the summit of the south bank of the Eske, in the parish of Lasswade, is situated the curious old baronial mansion of *Hawthornden*, the seat of William Drummond, the Scottish poet and historian, (who died in 1649,) and which is still the property of his descendants. Below the house, there is to be seen a set of ancient caves, cut out in the rock. The whole valley of the Eske is highly beautiful and picturesque.

NOTE C.

"Mid crowded obelisks and urns
I sought the untimely grave of Burns."

WORDSWORTH.

NOTE D.

Ellisland is beautifully situated on the south side of the Nith, some six miles above Dumfries. Here Burns wrote his "Tam o' Shanter," and many of his most admired songs.

NOTE E.

This refers to Mr. Anthony Yeoman, Surgeon, (from Dumfries-shire,) an amiable young man, with whom the author spent a pleasant week, in the winter of 1828–9, at Airth Castle, in the hospitable house of Mr. George Brown. Mr. Yeoman went into the Navy—but since that time I have never heard of him.

NOTE F.

The ruins of Buncle Castle, an ancient seat of the Stuart family, are seen at the foot of a range of hills called *Buncle Edge*—a little to the north of Buncle church. These hills were in old times covered with an extensive forest, which extended from Fosterland (famous in fairy-annals) on the east, to the Whitadder on the west. Along the summit of Buncle hills there can still be traced the remains of several old British entrenchments. Sir John Stuart of Buncle, a gallant warrior, fell in the battle of Falkirk in 1298.

NOTE G.

When Wallace " put Corspatrick out of Scotland," it is stated by *Harry the Minstrel*, that he visited Buncle Wood. I have therefore long reckoned the hills of Buncle consecrated ground, for I can say with Burns, that " the story of Wallace poured a Scottish prejudice into my veins, which will boil along there till the floodgates of life shut in eternal rest."

NOTE H.

At *Little Billy*, the scene of my birth, whose tall grey ash trees still leaning o'er its site, " were old a century before my day," an unfortunate woman hanged herself about 90 years ago, on one of the rafters of her house. She was buried in a marshy spot,—being denied, as was then the custom, " Christian burial,"—about a quarter of a mile to the south of the old hamlet. An old Rymer has *celebrated* this event in the following lines :—

" *Meg Landles* is lying by yon bog-side,
Where the lands o' *Billy* and *Lintlaw* meet ;
To an auld aik kipple she tied the rape,
And hung at its end, *wi' the deil at her feet*,
Till she was as dead as the nail in the door—
And they buried her like a dog therefore :
And a cairn o' stanes now lies on her banes,
And a willow tree waves by the loanin' green,
Where Maggie's grave may still be seen."

38

NOTE I.

Draedun is the name of a small stream on the farm of *Billy Mains*. On the south side of this stream, there existed a few years ago a large monumental cairn, and a tall upright stone at some little distance from the cairn, which was called " the Altar." This stone still stands, and it is supposed that this is the remnant of some ancient Druidical superstition, where human victims have bled and died.

NOTE K.

The most charming and picturesque history of Ruth the Moabitess cannot fail to leave a deep and lasting impression on every generous and sensitive bosom. It is enough to encourage every agriculturist to promote the practice of gleaning—a wise and benevolent practice which was inculcated upon the Jews as a law—and a practice which yet will be held as binding upon every humane husbandman. Surely it would be both more wise and creditable to proprietors and farmers, were they to allow the poor to glean after the reapers, than to scrape together a great mass of rubbish, stones, stubble, weeds, &c., with a large horse-rake, which has not inappropriately been termed *the Devil's Redding-kame*—and after all this scraping, and tearing together of such a quantity of rubbish, it is often left to remain in the fields till it is neither fit for man nor beast. But anything is better than to favour the poor. Our Established Clergy, in the lately published Statistical Accounts of their respective parishes, state that the poor are *now* far less reluctant to take advantage of the provision doled out to them by the Ministers and Heritors, than they were fifty years ago. This may be the fact—but they all attribute it to the wrong cause—to *a lower state of morals among the working classes, and to a deterioration of their manly and independent spirit.* Here our clergymen strain hard to propagate a desperate lie. These men are sure to chime in with the spirit of their patrons, and on all occasions they are ready to make themselves the sneaking, truckling, and slavish tools of the Aristocracy. The real cause of the poor being now more ready than formerly to apply for parish relief is this—*They have had every thing taken from them by the rich and powerful, on which, in past days, they relied for support in age and infirmity.* They are not now allowed to glean, as in old time. I have known an aged woman glean as much in harvest as would support her for one half of the year.—Their *commons* also have been seized upon by the harpies, where they frequently obtained their fuel, and food for their kine. Very few cottagers are allowed now to keep fowls, for fear of eating up the great man's corn. There is little or no spinning, carding, or knitting in country places now : these, and numerous other resources are cut off—and the poor people must either starve outright, or apply for the niggardly pittance from the parish funds. It is impossible that an independent spirit can survive in such circumstances—and what with bondage, incessant, hopeless labour, and starvation, our once " high-souled peasantry" must soon become a set of poor slavish serfs, unfit to perform any functions of men, except that of the labour of brutes.

39

NOTE L.

Billy Myre, which forms the northern boundary of the parish of Chirnside, is here alluded to. It is still said to be haunted by a ghost. *Billy Myre*, which lay in a long, narrow, singular valley, was only a few years since an impassable morass, except at one or two points—it is now all drained and cultivated.

NOTE M.

The ruins of *Billy* Castle lie in the south eastern part of the parish of Bunele. *Billy* was an ancient seat of the Earls of Angus, and here Archibald the 6th Earl resided in 1528, when he was in rebellion against his sovereign, and when his strong hold of *Tantallon* Castle was besieged by the king's forces—" Not willing," as Godscroft says, " to shut himself up within the walls of any strength, having ever in his mouth this maxime, (which he had received from his predecessours,) that *it was better to hear the lark sing than the mouse cheep.*"

NOTE N.

We here allude to the old obscure village of *Auchencrow*, famous in the annals of witchcraft, where the author spent a considerable portion of his school-boy days. *Auchencrow* was the birth-place of the enthusiastic *James Bonner*, author of a treatise on Bees—and where the inhabitants still have a penchant for the keeping of those valuable insects. Here also the famous Grecian, *John Strachan*, long kept a school. For several particulars concerning the *witches of Auchencrow*, we must refer the reader to a very curious MS. collection of rustic poetry, entitled " the Funny Rythmes of Auchencrow," now in our possession.

NOTE O.

As an illustrative Note to the description of *Chirnside*, perhaps it may not be out of place to subjoin a few extracts from a blank verse Epistle to a Friend, which the author wrote several years ago.

Would'st thou then know the beauties which surround
My dwelling-place? The scenes, and situation
Of the hamlets round me—and traditions old
Which float among the natives of the district?
Then know that this most rural-looking place
Which men call *Chirnside*, lies upon the road
'Twixt Dunse and Berwick old.

* * * * * *

From Chirnside hill a goodly prospect
Opens all around—to north and west
The pastoral slopes of Lammermoor arise ;
Conspicuous there is seen grey *Cockburn Law*,
And nearer still *Dunse-hill*, famous in annals
Of old Scotland's covenanted day ;

40

And farther on the west *Home's* castled height behold;
And in the distance blue, the hills and dales
Of bonny *Teviot-dale*;—and on the south,
Broad-stretching to the *Tweed* is seen
The level *Merse*, with all its groves and fields
Steep'd in the light of this sweet summer day:
And yonder rises *Norham's* hoary walls
Still frowning on the Tweed—with it
Associates many a deed of the rude times gone by;
And rising, on the Border-side, behold
The cloud-capp'd summit of old *Cheviot's* hill;
And *Flodden's* high and well-remembered field,
Where the rash James breathed out his martial soul
'Mong slaughter'd heaps of Scotia's daring sons,
Long mourn'd by Caledonia's daughters fair
In many a plaintive dirge.

* * * * * * *

Adjoining to our village, on the east,
Lie the fair lands and house of *Mains*,
Where lived the descendants of old *Mow*,
Who fell in border feud, on *Reidswire Edge*:—
Upon these lands, at their most southern point,
A *mineral*-spring out-gushes 'mong the sedge,
And flows into the neighbouring brook;
This fountain once was famous in the cure
Of scrofulous maladies, in bygone time,
And was resorted to by ailing people
Of the neighbouring towns—but now
'Tis fallen, like many a better cure
Into disuse: yet there the scene is lone and sweet,
And I have sat beside the well at summer noon,
Delighted and refreshed.

* * * * * *

Still further to the east, about a mile,
Is seen the shattered ruins of a baron's hold,
The castle of old *Edington*. Within its walls
In no far distant time the murderer *Lauder*
Dwelt, and held his dissolute sway.

South from the village lies *Whitehall*,
Surrounded with its lofty groves in summer verdure deck'd;
Here rooks do build and breed—and with their ceaseless din,
Heard at a distance, cheer my wayward heart;
Their cries are pleasing to my ear—
So also is the hooting of the owls, which here abound,
Heard at the midnight hour.
All Nature's sounds are pleasing, and delight
The heart not fashioned in the mint
Of Belial, or of Mammon.

* * * * * * *

41

Now farther on the west, whose park
Just stretches to the village, *Ninewells* stands,
O'erlooking pleasantly the glittering stream,
And shaded round with venerable trees ;
Here *David* the sophist, and historian, dwelt
Some years—here spinning his subtile fancies—
Vainly endeavouring to gainsay God's precious Word :—
David is gone, with all his dreary dreams ;
But bright as ever, burns the lamp of Truth,
And will burn on, till all have seen its light.

A few roods down the stream, there is a little holm
Close by the river, on its further side,
Which by the people here is called the *Chapel haugh ;*
Because a cell or chapel once stood here
In monkish times. This is a hallowed spot—
For here, in Scotland's evil day, when Prelacy
With rampant bigotry the gospel-spirit spurn'd,
And at a king's behest tried to impose a hated creed
Upon a free-born race, and bind their consciences
To that which they abhorr'd—for who but God
Is umpire of the conscience ?—where's the right
Of kings and prelates to make creeds and forms
Unto the Church of Christ ? Yes ! here is sacred ground ;
For here in Scotland's evil day a great conventicle
Was held, where thousands of the persecuted ones
Listened in ecstasy unto the preached Word,
By Welch, Rae, Dickson, Blackadder, and Riddel,
Who spoke like men inspired, beneath the summer sky,
Unto the multitude, who on the green brae-side
Sat all entranced in serious awe :—watchmen were set
Upon the neighbouring heights to sound the alarm
Should any wicked foe intrude upon the solemn scene ;
But God withheld the enemies' hand *that* day ;
And none disturb'd the pious worshippers :
The water gently rippled past, glittering in the sun,
And all the air was still, serene, and warm ;
On every side the little hills rejoiced ;
And bird and beast seem'd more than usual glad.
Upon that day, more than three thousand souls
Vowed to be Christ's, and Christ's alone,
At the communion-table, by the water side ;
Few days like *that* were e'er in Scotland seen—
A glorious day of Nature, and the Son of Man !
When evening's lengthened shadows o'er the dewy earth
Were stretch'd, how sweet it was to hear
The solemn, pensive, parting song of praise !
From thousand voices swelling on the air,
And echoing far o'er bushy bank and dell !

42

To those who listened on the hill, no melody
Was e'er so sweet and plaintive as the parting song
Of that great multitude. 'Tis ended,
And the people lingeringly disperse
All to their several homes. Many from far
Came to the great solemnity, and through the dewy night
They travell'd to their distant homes,
Enjoying converse sweet; their hearts
Burning within them by the way;
And long remembered by both young and old,
In Scotia's lowly turf-built dwellings,
Were all the sacred and divine delights
Of *Nesbit's* great communion.

* * * * * * *

Above the *Chapel-haugh,* upon a promontory
Form'd by the circuit of the rippling stream,
Was seen, in former years, a Roman camp
Made by the conquerors of the world
In ancient days, when Britain was a wild
Uncultivated land of marshes deep and forests vast:
But *now* no traces of this camp are seen,
For over it the plough has frequent gone;
And yellow corn waved o'er the trenches all.
And has the Roman soldier stood upon these banks,
And viewed the sister rivers join their streams,
Where yonder pleasant village stands upon the steep,
And where these busy mills their dusty labours ply?
Yes! there he stood, a lonely sentinel,
And thought, with heavy heart, upon his native land,
The fair Italia!

* * * * * *

Thus we have old remembrances, and prospects fair;
Rich fields of waving grain, and pastures green;
Old shady groves, fair seats, and flowery banks,
Clear streams, and fountains pure,
Fit haunts for musing poet, or lovers fond!"

* * * * * *

43

STANZAS

TO THE

MEMORY OF MY FIRST-BORN,

WHO DIED OF HOOPING COUGH, OCTOBER 11, 1839,
AGED ONE YEAR AND EIGHT MONTHS.

Oh, she was lovely, good, and fair,
Unstricken by the shafts of care,
Fell sorrow came not near her:
Meek as the lamb that crops the lea,
Sweet as the blossom on the tree—
No child was ever dearer!

The rose ne'er wore a lov'lier hue
Than did the lips and cheeks embue
Of my belov'd and sweetest;
Her brow was like the lily fair,
Around her was an angel air—
In face and form completest!

Still lively as the summer bee,
Her artless ways were sweet to see,
Her smile shed bliss before us;
Her eyes, two sparkling gems of light,
Dispell'd the phantoms of affright
That sometimes hover'd o'er us!

44

No merrier laugh was ever heard,
To ring through dwelling of a bard,
When high her spirits bounded;
She met us with unrivall'd glee,
And clamb with joy her father's knee,
And forth her pleasure sounded!

No whimpering fretful elf she was,
To whine or cry without a cause;
Even when disease assail'd her,
She lay, like lambkin taking rest,
Though pain'd and sore her little breast,
Her patience never fail'd her.

But fairest flowers are frail, they say,
And soonest droop and fade away
Before the stormy weather;—
And thou, the fairest human flower,
Hast sunk before death's chilling power,
That round thee soon did gather.

God saw thy fragile form in time,
Ill fitted for earth's blighting clime,
And snatch'd thee from all danger;
Transplanting thee to regions blest—
There thou wilt blossom 'mong the best;
To glory now no stranger.

To us she was the richest dower
That e'er could bless our lowly bower,
The sweet, the fair departed!
We give thee to thy God again,
Though all our hopes of thee are slain,
And we are weary-hearted.

45

Though here no more my child I'll meet,
Methinks, I still should hear so sweet
Her clear glad voice resounding!
Illusions vain!—my heart I cheat,
For never more her pattering feet
Shall o'er our floor go bounding!

We'll miss her sore, at close of day,
When on our hearth she used to play,
And cheer our hours of sorrow;
No more we'll kiss her lips so sweet,
And feel her happy bosom beat,
At either night or morrow!

The mother oft will dream of thee,
And smile thy fairy-form to see
Beside some fount or river;
She'll clasp again her wandering dove
With all a yearning mother's love,
That fails or falters never.

But oh, as soon as she has ta'en
Her lost one to her heart again,
The blissful vision's shattered—
She starts, and weeps with bleeding breast
For thee, the fairest, first, and best,
And all her hopes are scatter'd!

But since to us she'll ne'er come back,
We follow fast her grave-ward track;—
In Heaven could we but reach her!
Unscathed by sin, and pain, and woe,
And far from earth's vain, gilded show,
She sees the Lord—the Teacher!

46

When tired in heart, and tired in limb,
The world's rugged paths I climb,
I want her smile to cheer me;
When sick of earth's delusive wiles,
Its dark deceit, and faithless smiles,
I wish that she were near me!

Her beauteous head in earth is thrust,
Her fair hair dabbl'd in the dust—
How still and cold she slumbers!—
A little way she's gone before,
And reach'd the Jordan's farthest shore,
To swell Emmanuel's numbers!

She walks the spirit's flowery land,
Among yon happy angel band,
The Fount of Life is near her!
For ever, and for evermore,
The God of Love she'll there adore,
No woful sight to fear her!

I go not to her grave to weep,
Though tears my eyelids oft will steep—
I go not there to find her;
Her spirit, on the wings of love,
Has reach'd the blessed land above,
All earth is cast behind her!

The grass shall wave above her head,
And rain and snow be o'er her shed
For seasons and for ages;
But where her nobler part has gone
Is never utter'd sigh or groan,
And there no winter rages.

47

Then let us here a farewell take
Of giddy scenes for her dear sake,
That AGNES there may meet us;
Come, let us tread God's righteous ways,
And shun the world's entangling maze,
Which will for ever cheat us.

We'll wander on, though sore in heart,
Since she from these dim scenes did part,
They look more dark and dreary;
But though from earth she's ta'en her flight,
She *lives* in scenes for ever bright—
That thought inspires the weary!

On the damp earth, before the blast,
Pale Autumn's wither'd leaves are cast,
Types of frail life, I ponder;
But they who sit by Life's fair tree,
In love and light shall ever be—
No change can reach them yonder!

Let courage then our bosoms cheer,
While onward through life's seas we steer,
The haven lies before us;
Toil, scorn, and grief, we here endure,
But Faith to rest will guide us sure—
Spread, Lord, thy blessing o'er us!

Chirnside, Nov. 4, 1839.

48

NATURE'S CHARMS.

"Consider the lilies of the field, how they grow:—even Solomon, in all his glory, was not arrayed like one of these."

St. Matthew.

In verdant dells, remote and lone,
I love to muse, and wander on
By ferny tuft, and mossy stone,
And fountain clear,
Where Nature's gems are lavish strewn
From year to year.

I love to hear the wood-bird's lay,
Wild-warbled from the hazel spray,
At dawning morn or close of day,
In freedom sweet,
Amidst the leaves and blooms of May,
When lambkins bleat.

By shaded rill I love to lie
And gaze upon the azure sky,
While soft the waters murmur by
Below the tree,
And far is heard the lapwing's cry
From misty lea.

49

How sweet the cuckoo's mellow note
Come's o'er the dewy hill remote,
While bleating flocks, by upland cot
Awake the morn!
And fragrance on the air doth float
From blossom'd thorn.

And fair the fox-glove's speckled bell
Waves in the deep, romantic dell,
Where wild bees build their mossy cell,
And gather sweets
From all the blooming buds that swell
In green retreats.

Sweet is the sloe-thorn's rugged copse,
And sweet the sunny, grassy slopes,
Where oft I've lain and nourish'd hopes
In Fancy's sight,
And fed my heart with honey'd drops
Of Heaven's delight.

Though gold and grandeur be not mine,
Nor fortune's favours on me shine;
For these my heart shall never pine
While Nature smiles,
To give my soul a joy divine
'Midst cares and toils.

Let wealth and power in all their pride
The poor man's state and gifts deride;
Yet in this faith I'll still abide—
That Nature's glee
Gives more delight than dukedom's wide,
To all who're free.

E

50

The gowan fresh from vernal shower,
The wood-sorrel's pale and drooping flower,
The anemone in forest bower,
My heart doth sway
More than all worldly wealth or power,
By night or day.

The hare-bell blue, in bushy glade,
The violet brooding in the shade,
The cowslip's drooping cups inlaid
With spots of gold,
Bring to my bosom thoughts arrayed
In magic's mould.

The globe-flower's yellow nodding gem,
Richer than monarch's diadem,
The meadow's-queen on taller stem,
So scented sweet,
Bring back my early days with them,
Whene'er we meet.

And who can view the broom's array,
With gorgeous flowers on bank and brae,
And wild rose blooming to the day
Above the burn,
And never feel sweet Nature's sway
His bosom turn?

Yes! turn from Fashion's apish train,
From all the paltry paths of gain,
And selfish aims which leave a stain
Of darkest dye
On worldly hearts, proud, silly, vain,
Who sunken lie.

51

Leave lucre to the grovelling crew,
And be thou still to Nature true,
Wend forth her endless charms to view
By stream and wood,
And thou wilt find creation through
All very good.

By reedy fen, or sedge-crown'd rill,
O'er moorland dun, and breezy hill,
Where hoary cairns are brooding still
O'er slaughter'd wight,
Come wander forth, thy breast to fill
With visions bright.

The lowly milkwort blooms again,
With butterwort of azure stain,
To lure us to the pastoral plain,
Or dank marsh low,
Where marigolds, like maidens vain,
Their beauties show.

Then far from crowds and cities haste,
And roam with me the uncultur'd waste,
And Nature's odorous beauties taste
In moor and glen,
And there your sorrows shall be chas'd
Beyond your ken.

'Tis sweet to lie by mossy well,
Beside the blooming asphodel,
Or search the heath that skirts the dell
For berries blae,
Where the green fox-tail decks the fell
With lichens grey.

52

I love the cup-moss, crimson tipt,
The splendid orchis, purple-lipp'd,
The wild-thyme where the bee hath sipp'd
A precious drop;
And emerald rings where fairies tripp'd,
Give Fancy scope.

But sweeter far I love the flower
Scatter'd on moorlands, Flora's dower—
Grass of Parnassus!—bless'd the power
That made thee mine
In boyhood's blooming, happy hour,
When all was fine!

And let me perish, if the day
Should e'er arrive, when Nature's sway
Shall o'er my heart and soul decay,
If flower or tree,
Or bird, or insect fade away
In charms to me!

In all that flies, or swims, or grows,
In tiniest moss, or full-blown rose,
In rain or dew, or wind that blows
God's hand we trace,
And everything his goodness shows
In every place.

53

LINES

WRITTEN BY THE MONUMENT OF THE REV. HENRY ERSKINE, IN CHIRNSIDE CHURCHYARD, ON AUGUST 5TH, 1839.

No sycophant to wriggle, smile, and fawn
On bloated wealth, insatiate power, and pride,
Or shape his manners to smooth Fashion's tide
Lies here below:—an honest, upright man
Was *Henry Erskine!*—bright his course he ran,
And ne'er the truth, for fear of man, could hide:
Built on the Rock of Faith, he took the gospel plan,
Though persecution's fiends did o'er him ride,
And hunted him from house and home. But who
Rais'd o'er his dust this monumental pile?—
The Cameronians!—they who *once* were true,
And stood alone unus'd to flattering style,
The stern sons of the Covenant, who ne'er yielded jot
Of creed, or faith, unto the men in power:
But *now* alas! their former love's forgot,
And *now* they suit their fashion to the hour;
The state-created church *they* court with purpose vain,
And dally with her charms, and all her gilded train!—
In their new paramour let them delight,
And lick the feet that o'er their fathers trode!
Let them go on, and swell Corruption's might!—
But Truth ne'er loves to take a crooked road;

54

And *Erskine*—he for whom this stone was rear'd,
Would scorn'd to have been by sycophants revered;
Were he alive, *he'd* shun their sneaking crime,
And spurn all those who're *servers of the time.*

NOTE.

Mr. Henry Erskine was the first Presbyterian Minister of Chirnside, after the Revolution. He died on 10th August, 1696, aged 72 years. He is well known as the father of the two eminent individuals, *Ralph* and *Ebenezer Erskine*, the fathers and founders of the *Secession Church* of Scotland. He suffered, in his time, much hardship and persecution for his non-conformity to Prelacy, from the mad high churchmen of those days, who had the ruling power in their hands. The following Enigmatical Epitaph, said to be the composition of the *Rev. John Dysert* of Coldingham, who was Erskine's contemporary, and a man of somewhat kindred spirit, is still to be seen on the original throuch placed on his grave :—

" Beneath this stone there lies a stone,
" Living with God above,
" Built on the Rock was such a one
" Whom force nor fraud could move."

The Monument, to which the lines refer, was erected by subscription in 1820, and it bears the following appropriate inscription :—

" In memory of the Reverend Henry Erskine, a descendant of the family of Mar, and sometime Minister of this Parish, who was eminently distinguished by incorruptible integrity in private life, undaunted zeal in the service of his Heavenly Master, and steady attachment to the religious principles of the Church of Scotland, at a time when the profession of those principles often led to imprisonment and exile, both which he himself endured with exemplary resignation and fortitude.

" He was born at Dryburgh in the year 1624, ordained at Cornhill 1649, ejected in 1662, and persecuted for non-conformity to Prelacy; admitted soon after the Revolution in 1688, to be Minister of Chirnside, where he continued in the faithful discharge of his pastoral duties till 10th August, 1696, when his holy and exemplary life terminated in a peaceful and triumphant death, in the 72d year of his age, and 17th of his Ministry."

It is proper to state that men of all parties united to raise the present monument in memory of one so highly meritorious—but the subscription was principally planned and promoted, if we are correctly

55

informed, by a worthy and distinguished member of the *Cameronian* Church—and through his influence chiefly the monument was erected —which does credit alike to the architect, and the author of the inscription. This monument was raised, as has been already stated, in 1820, at an expense of £33. At that time, the Cameronians spoke a different language than they do at present, in respect to our Ecclesiastical institutions. There are men of supple pliant natures, who have a knack of turning their coats, in conformity to the fashion of the times. It is honourable however to many of them, that they do not approve of the Erastian doctrine of a Church and State alliance—and of course cannot acquiesce in the present proceedings of their ministers, and chief men, in respect to old mother Church. It is certainly a singular feature of Cameronianism, at this time of day, to see them claiming kindred with our present Church establishments, and bending down their souls to those puppets of the state, and giving what political power they possess into the hands of the rampant Tories—who may justly be considered the representatives of those bloody men who so bitterly persecuted their fathers in the days of old. There is something excessively degrading in joining the senseless, bigoted, and delusive howl of the Tories—"The Church in danger!"—"No Popery"—"Church Extension"—"Non-Intrusion," &c. It is very like a concert of jackasses. And shall Cameronians engage in the dirty work of the Church in this way! This is one of the wonders of the age, set up, we suppose, to counteract that "spurious liberalism," and "*ignis-fatuus*" spirit, which prevails so much in our day among dissenters, papists, and infidels, and which is so galling to a pampered priesthood, and to all those who have learned to *march backward*, to the tune of "Church-and-State for ever!" To make the Church of Christ dependant on acts of Parliament—to appoint a pensioned and state-endowed clergy—men nominated and thrust in on the people by patrons and presbyteries, so as to render them independent of the flocks to whom they minister—are certainly the greatest enormities that were ever practised on earth. No plan is surely better calculated to secularize the clergy, and to cheat the people out of their most valuable rights and privileges: but "a brighter light than that of the sun, hath dawned upon the nations," and a way is opening up for a great reformation! Every patriotic and unprejudiced mind must hail these favourable appearances with delight and rapture.

56

SONNETS.

TO EBENEZER ELLIOT, OF SHEFFIELD, THE CORN-LAW RHYMER.

I.

Thou, of the noble heart and manly brow,
Whom despots hate, and sons of pride despise!
To thee the poor look up with hopeful eyes,
And pray that blessings of all kinds may grow
Around thy happy home. To thee they breathe the vow
Of love and warm regard, and gaze upon the skies,
Believing that their Father sees their agonies,
And will for ever bless the Bard, who battles for them now.
Poet of the lowly virtuous, and the toil-worn men,
Whom princes tax, and lordlings grind to dust!
Thousands of British hearts revere thy burning pen,
And feel thy strains inspire their souls with trust,
With hope and courage bold. Oh Patriot brave and free!
Accept this lay from one, who tyrants hates like thee.

II.

O may thy strains arouse the careless, cold, and dead,
Who slumber in their chains unconscious of the thrill
Which burns in freemen's hearts—and may'st thou fill
Their souls with noble ire to spurn the despot's tread;
And may the sweat that from their brows distil
Never be pour'd, that bread-tax lords may feed
Upon their toil-wrung gains—may thy harp ne'er be still
Till Freedom's banner on the winds of Heaven
Proclaims that Britain's sons are free from thrall,
When they shall toil untax'd, and eat the bread that's given
With thankfulness and joy, to God who giveth all—
Be strong thy heart and hands, dear Elliot! evermore,
And loved thy noble strains while oceans lave the shore.

June 8th, 1836.

57

SOLITUDE.

I love to wander in untrodden ways,
And lie reclined in sunny grassy nooks,
Where Nature sweet her floral wealth displays
By gushing fountains and meandering brooks,
Where no wise-worldly soul upon me looks,
To mock my joys, or at my pursuits jeer;
Where my companions are the jays and rooks,
And round me smile the glories of the year
In bud and bloom. There rise the odorous flowers!
Those lovely gems which 'scap'd the curse of sin,
And hither came from Eden's glorious bowers,
To give to man some glimpse of that within
The heavenly land, that lies beyond the grave,
Where amaranthine blooms Life's river aye doth lave.

ON HEARING THE LARK SINGING, 9TH FEBRUARY, 1837.

Praise God, my soul!—I've heard the lark again—
The cheerful, soaring songster of the spring,
Escaped from winter's chilling snow and rain,
Back to my heart doth hope and gladness bring—
Mount, mount thou lovely bird! and blithely fling
Thy melody into the sky, and chase the pain
That long has wrung my soul!—To-day thy wing
Is gilded with the gladdening sun, and thy sweet strain
Is sorrowless. O could I mount with thee
Above the cold damp earth, and leave my woe
Behind!—and filled with joy and glee
O that my heart with love would overflow;
And fann'd with the fresh mountain breezes free,
I'd soar above the clouds, and thy companion be!

58

SPRING.

God's goodness still endures!—He makes the spring return,
And winter wild relax his rage—fresh breezes blow,
And glittering in the sun, the waters purer flow;
The buds are swelling green on hazel, birch and thorn,
And snow-white blossoms deck the leafless sloe.
I saw among the moss, beside the wimpling burn,
A primrose tuft in bloom, and by the river, lo!
The butter-burr hath burst in blossom from its urn.
Now forth I'll go again and seek the violet's haunts
Beneath the hedge or by the woodland glade;
I'll watch the yellow bee supply her vernal wants
From silver willow-buds, or furze, so rich arrayed.
With fresh delight and joy, each thing in Nature pants,
And new and pleasant hopes in mortal hearts are made.

NATURE.

All flowers, and insects, rivers, and green trees,
Clouds of the sky, and changes of the moon,
The howling winds in Autumn's forests brown,
The lightnings fierce, and raging of the seas,
All o'er my heart bring various phantasies
In every season round—when Spring does crown
The earth with blossoms sweet, and down
The Summer smiles upon the daisied leas.
In all my walks and wanderings I behold
A kind hand lavishing its stores on earth,
Arraying insects' wings in green and gold,
Teaching the birds to utter forth their mirth,
And feeding man and beast with blessings manifold,
That gratitude sincere may in our souls have birth.

59

WRITTEN IN DULAW DEAN, NEAR FAST CASTLE, IN JULY, 1835.

This glen is wild, and savage, lone, and deep,
Its shattered rocks are all with lichen grey,
And prickly brambles o'er their fragments stray;
The ivy green waves on the giddy steep,
And hawthorns hoar their nooks of shelter keep;
The lowly rose-wort decks the rugged brae,
The dark green alder o'er the brook doth weep,
And the tall willow-herb its rosy flowers display.
How sweet a place it is for hermit, or for bard
To sit on some rude cliff above the water's fall,
Where the loud voice of ocean's waves are heard,
And muse on Nature's work, so wondrous all!
Such lone recess I love, far from men's haunts debarr'd,
And feel my heart refresh'd from care and sorrow's thrall.

TO A FRIEND.

Be not afraid, when prosperous and successful men
Shall mock and jeer thee in triumphant scorn—
Hold on thy course though poor and lowly born;
Though all the devils from their sulphurous den,
And Mammon's sordid crew to lucre sworn,
Exult and gnash their teeth in thousands ten
O'er thee and thine!—yet feel not thou forlorn,
Nor hopeless sink in sorrow's dreary fen.
Keep still the virtuous path, and ne'er be once afraid,
Though Fashion's kailworm sons deride thee;
And though through slander's foul streams thou must wade
Let not the mist of misanthropy hide thee;
But be thy heart in truth and charity for ever staid,
And then the God of truth will ever guide thee!

60

SONNET—INSCRIBED TO BETTY B——— AN OLD HYPOCRITICAL, GOSSIPING, AND SLANDEROUS HAG!

Loathsome as putrid corpse, half-rotten in the clay,
Foul as a common-sewer where every filth is thrown,
Vile as a nauseous dunghill with putrescence strewn,
Loathly as efts and toads, from which all turn away,
Poisonous as nightshade, whose red fruits betray;
Fell as dark hemlock by the pathway side!
And deadly as the viper's cruelest tooth,
Are the vile slanderous words which glide
From thy smooth tongue, with great delight, in sooth!
Blasting with fiendish breath the virtue and the truth
That squares not with thy phraizing, fawning way,
And gloating o'er all blight, without a touch of ruth—
Go, thou foul hag!—bound under Satan's sway,
And slaver forth deceit, till he thy old hide flay!

March, 1839.

The Author has ready for the Press the following productions:—

1. ANTIQUARIAN and BOTANICAL EXCURSIONS in the EASTERN PART of BERWICKSHIRE. To which is added, the Proverbs, Rythmes, &c., peculiar to the County.
2. FRAGMENTS of THOUGHTS and FEELINGS.
3. WAYSIDE FANCIES—consisting of Short Poems and Sonnets on several occasions.
4. The FEAST of the RIVER GENII, and other Poems.
5. MEMOIRS of a COUNTRY SURGEON—consisting of Letters, Journals, Notes, &c., in the daily Journey of Life.
6. NOCTES CHIRNSIDIS; or, Nights in Chirnside.

Glossary

aits, oats
aiver, old horse
aivers, eager fellows
aneuch, enough
ask, newt
auld farrant, old-fashioned
aumries, cupboards
ava', at all
awin' owing
bandster, binder of corn sheaves
barkimt, tanned leather
bastle, fortress
bausie, big fat horse
bausuit, white-faced
beckin', curtseying
begouk, deceive
bere, barley
bield, shlter
bien, well-off
birkie, smart conceited lad
birses, bristles
birst, challenge, effort
blaw, boast
blirty, sudden
blitter, snipe
blythesome, joyful
bole, window hole
boon, happily
bore the gree, held first place
bour tree, elder tree
bouser, boozer
bowdy, bandy-legged
braid, broad
brose, oatmeal, peasemeal
bught, sheep-milking fold
bum, to rush
bur, bur-reed
busk, dress up
buskit, dressed up
ca' canny, be careful
ca't a' your ain, call it all your own
caller, fresh
cantle, crown (of head)
cantrips, spells, tricks
carl, male witch
cast, fall
cauldrife, chilly
causey, causeway
chimla-taps, chimney pots
claggy, sticky
clout, cloth
cluds, clouds
con, learn by heart
cot, cottage
craik, crake, corncrake
crambo strain, rhyming doggerel
cranreuch, hoar frost
crone, old woman

crousely, boldly, cheerfully
cuds, cuddies, donkeys
curly-doddy, ribwort plantain
cushet, wood pigeon
daiver'd, stunned
dern, hiding
dings a', beats all
dinnae, don't
douce, quiet, sober, gentle
dowie, sad, dismal
dowp, backside
dree, bear, suffer, endure
droukit, soaked, drenched
drouthy, thirsty
drucken, drunken
dub, puddle
dummer, dumbfound
durst, dared
elrich, weird
Ercildoun, Earlston
fauld, fold
fegs, in faith
flags, irises
flaughts, flakes
foss, ditch
frae, from
fremmit, foreign
frith, firth
fushionless, feeble, useless
ga', gall
gabbie, blether
gabs, blethers
gaen gyte, gone crazy
gair, a patch of land
gairy, gaudy
gar, make, force
girn, grumble
girnin', grimacing, snarling
glarry, muddy
gley'd, squint-eyed
glitty, slimy
gloaming, dusk
goam, recognise
goun, gown
gowan, daisy; ox-eye daisy
grane, groan
gree, rank, degree
groffle, grovel
groflin', grovelling
grubble, srruggle
guller, roar
gumflowers, artificial flowers
gurl, growl
gyte, mad, crazy
haffet lock, ringlet
hag, swamp hole
hap, wrap up, cover
hare-bell, the Scots bluebell
haud, hold
haugh, riverside meadow
havers, nonsensical talk
heigh, high
hempy, roguish, rough
het, hot, heated
hie, high
hirsel, flock; sheepfold
horse-couper, horse dealer
houkit, dug up
howe, hollow
howk, dig up
humlock, hummock
ilka, each; every
illfard, ugly
ingle, fireside
John Barleycorn, whisky
kail, cabbage broth
kempin', competing
kenn'd, known

kent, known
kent, shepherd's staff
kirn, churn
kirn, harvest-home
knaggie, peg, hook
knowe, hillock
kye, cows; cattle
labbs, bits and pieces
lair'd, sank in the mud
laits, manners, habits
lap, cover
laverock, skylark
leal, loyal, honest
leister, salmon spear
lilt, song
limmer, rogue, thief
lint, flax
lintie, linnet
lint-locks, flaxen hair
lintwhite, linnet
lirk, crease, wrinkle
loach, a freshwater fish
loon, lad
lound, peaceful, sheltered
louns, lads
loup, leap over
lugs, ears
lyart pow, grey hair
maen, moan
Mahoun, the devil
maist, most
'mang, among
maud, cloak
maun, must
mauten'd, mouldy
mead, meadow
meadow queen, meadowsweet
mensfu, hospitable
merle, blackbird
minnon, minnow
mony, many
mooter/multure, tax paid to millers
muckle skate, silly fool
muckle, much, big
nags, horses
neist, next
norlin', northern
nowte, cattle
orrie, ordinary, everyday
paddock, frog; toad
parritch-kettle, porridge pot
peesweep, peewit; lapwing
pirn, prank
plack, an old Scots coin
plet, plait
plet, plaited
pleting, plaiting
pleugh, plough
plew'd, ploughed
polypody, a kind of fern
poortith, poverty
posy, savings, valuables
pow, head
puddock, frog or toad
raeme, rhyme
rattan, din
rede, read
reeky, smoky
reiver, cattle raider
remead, remedy
rig, strip of ploughed land
rip, loose stalks of corn
rowes, rolls
rowth, abundance
rudous, cantankerous
sair, sore
sark, shirt
saugh, willow

saugh-buss, willow-bush
saut, salt
scoup, bound, caper
screed, tear, rent
scrievin, swift-moving
sea-mews, seagulls
segg, sedge
shairn, muck, dung
shaw, a small wood
shiel, shieling, hut, house
shilfa, chaffinch
shock, stook
Shursit, Chirnside
sic, such
siller, silver; money; wealth
skyte, to brush off
slae, sloe
slap, gap, hill pass
slee tyke, sly, boorish person
slooming, slipping
smoor, smother,
snell, sharp, keen
snoove, to slink
sock o' the plough, plough blade
sonsie queans, buxom lassies
soughing, moaning, sighing
spank, move nimbly, briskly
spunk, ember, candle-end
spunkies, spirits, ghosts
stank, ditch
steerie, commotion
stibble, stubble
stiltin', stalking
stobs, thorns
stoited, stotted
stoiterin', staggering
stook, shock of cut corn sheaves
stoon, occasion
stoun, stupefying din
stound, din, shock
stour, dust
strae, straw
straikit, smoothed
swarf, faint, swoon
swatter, splashing
sweer, loth
swinglin', beating
swithers, doubts, indecisions
taed, toad
tarry-breeks, a sailor
tedd, spread out to dry
theekit, thatched
thrapple, throat
thraw, wring
tint, lost, mistook
tocher, dowry
toom, empty
troke, business, deals
tyke, dog, cur
tyne, lose
unco, very
wabster, weaver
wae, sad
wae, woe
waesome, woesome
wair'd, drained
wampussin', moving jauntily
waur, worse
wecht, corn basket
weir, war
whittle, sheath-knife
wight, fellow
yaud, old horse
yell-wife, ale-wife
yill, ale
yirn, curdle
yirth, earth
yont, beyond

Bibliography

Allan, John S., *My Picture Gallery of Memory* (1970, North Berwick, Tantallon Press)

Berwick Advertiser (1840–1864)

Berwickshire Mss, Vols 1–3 (transcriptions of parts of the unpublished mss journals of Dr George Henderson. Ref SBA/265 Scottish Borders Archive)

Crockett, W. S., *Minstrelsy of the Merse: the Poets and Poetry of Berwickshire; a County Anthology* (1893, Paisley, J. & R. Parlane)

Henderson, George, *The Scenes of Boyhood; and other Poems* (1840, Berwick, C. Richardson)

Henderson, George, *The Popular Rhymes, Sayings, and Proverbs of the County of Berwick; with illustrative notes* (1856, Newcastle upon Tyne, W. S. Crow)

Henderson George, *Nugae Medici* (unpublished ms as quoted by W. S. Mitchell q.v.)

History of the Berwickshire Naturalists' Club (1831–present)

Hunt, Erica, *Chirnside Past and Present* (1975, Chirnside)

MacLeod, Dawn, *Land of Tweed* (1983, Edinburgh, Blackwood)

Mitchell, W. S., 'Dr George Henderson of Chirnside (1800–1864)', in *Medical History* Vol. 5, July 1961

Rogers, Charles, *The Modern Scottish Minstrel, Vol. VI* (1857, Edinburgh, A. & C. Black)

Watson, James, *Living Bards of the Border* (1859, Edinburgh, Paton & Ritchie)